Cricket
THE GREAT BOWLERS

Cricket
THE GREAT BOWLERS

*Studies of
Ten Great Bowlers
of Cricket History*

*

GENERAL EDITOR

John Arlott

PELHAM BOOKS

First published in Great Britain by
PELHAM BOOKS LTD
26 *Bloomsbury Street*
*London, W.C.*1
1968

© 1968 *by Bagenal Harvey Organisation*

7207 0187 2

Set and printed in Great Britain by
Tonbridge Printers Ltd, Peach Hall Works, Tonbridge, Kent
in Times ten on twelve point, and bound by
James Burn at Esher, Surrey

PREFACE

It was Alec Bedser who, after one of his seasons of mighty labour, remarked drily 'The last bowler to be knighted was Francis Drake'. Certainly it has generally been batsmen who have drawn the crowds – W. G., Victor Trumper; Sir Jack Hobbs, Sir Donald Bradman, Denis Compton, or the hitters like Jessop and Sir Learie Constantine.

The bowlers, however, have not been without their admirers: crowds came specially to watch bowlers – usually the fast men – Gregory and McDonald, Larwood, Constantine, Lindwall and Miller, Statham, Trueman and Tyson; but also some of the spinners – Grimmett and O'Reilly, Ramadhin and Valentine in their amazing summer of 1950, Laker and Lock and, in Wales, Clay, Muncer and Trick in Glamorgan's Championship year.

The problem here was never one of which bowlers to include, but which to leave out. These are not quite the greatest bowlers, for Wilfred Rhodes – who took more wickets than anyone else – has his place in another volume, on all-rounders: so have Constantine, Miller, Hirst, Benaud and Sobers. Two extra were achieved by including, in the eight studies, the pairings of Grimmett and O'Reilly, Trueman and Statham.

Turner and Ferris – never to be separated – Spofforth, Tom Richardson, Lockwood and Lohmann, Peel, Peate and Trumble were all excluded because no living writer can speak from first-hand experience of them in their heyday. Others had strong claims to inclusion – Ramadhin and Valentine – but their effective career at top level was short – Tayfield, Farnes, Bill Johnston, Gregory and McDonald, Bosanquet, Hedley Verity: but their peers lie within the compass of this series, and who should have been left out for them?

Each writer has a special knowledge of and interest in his subject: but their approaches, from the severely practical to the warmly felt, are, I believe, sufficiently different to give variety.

Once again, an appendix gives each player's career in statistics. This book may not compensate for the unbestowed knighthoods but it is a tribute to high achievement and true greatness.

NOTES ON THE CONTRIBUTORS

Sir Neville Cardus: born Manchester, 1889: as 'Cricketer' of *The Manchester Guardian* he virtually created the modern – 'appreciation' – and cricket writing. Now music and cricket critic of *The Guardian*, he is the author of some of the most graceful and gracious books about cricket, several musical studies and two lively volumes of autobiography. Knighted 1967.

A. A. Thomson: born Harrogate, 1894: President of the Cricket Society: one of the kindest and most appreciative of cricket writers, with an ear for anecdote and a feeling for character. Has written some dozen books on cricket, several novels, and biographies: a felicitous after-dinner speaker. Died 1968.

W. E. – Bill – Bowes: born Elland, Yorkshire, 1908: fast bowler for M.C.C., Yorkshire and England, 1928 to 1947: cricket correspondent of *The Yorkshire Evening Post*: author of an autobiography, *Express Deliveries*, and two tour accounts: a close and informed observer of cricket, he was a member of the M.C.C. party to Australia in 1932–33 which saw Larwood at his greatest.

I. A. R. – Ian – Peebles: born Aberdeen, 1908: leg-break and googly bowler for Oxford University, Middlesex, Scotland and England, 1928 to 1939: cricket correspondent of *The Sunday Times*. Author of several anecdotal and perceptive books about cricket and cricketers, he had played cricket, and observed its players, in four continents.

Ray Robinson: born Sydney, 1908: the most distinguished contemporary Australian cricket writer and a close observer of the cricketing scene there for almost forty years; Australian correspondent of *The Cricketer, The Times, The Observer* and author of three outstanding cricket books of recent years from Australia – all written in an original 'hard' – style – *Between Wickets, From the Boundary* and *The Glad Season*.

John Woodcock: born Longparish, Hampshire, 1926: wicketkeeper for Oxford Authentics, Free Foresters, M.C.C., and Longparish; Oxford Hockey Blue; Cricket correspondent *The Man-*

chester Guardian* 1952 to 1954, *The Times* 1954 to date: the most significant of the new generation of English cricket writers.

John Arlott: born Basingstoke, Hampshire 1914: has written and broadcast about cricket since 1946.

Frank Tyson: born Middleton, Lancashire, 1930: fast bowler for Northants and England 1952 to 1960: author of autobiography *A Typhoon Called Tyson*: schoolmaster in Melbourne, Australian cricket correspondent to several English magazines and newspapers: television commentator in Australia.

Michael Fordham: born Faversham, Kent, 1926: local government officer: statistician to the *Playfair Cricket Monthly, Playfair Cricket Annual,* and for The Gillette Cup: editor of *Cricket Records*: scorer for B.B.C.

CONTENTS

PREFACE	5
NOTES ON CONTRIBUTORS	7
S. F. BARNES *by Sir Neville Cardus*	13
MAURICE TATE *by A. A. Thomson*	35
HAROLD LARWOOD *by Bill Bowes*	59
GRIMMETT and O'REILLY *by Ian Peebles*	81
RAY LINDWALL *by Ray Robinson*	101
ALEC BEDSER *by John Woodcock*	121
JIM LAKER *by John Arlott*	137
TRUEMAN and STATHAM *by Frank Tyson*	157
Statistics *by Michael Fordham*	175

ILLUSTRATIONS

S. F. Barnes	*facing page* 32
Maurice Tate	33
Harold Larwood	64
C. V. Grimmett	65
W. J. O'Reilly	96
Ray Lindwall	97
Alec Bedser	128
Jim Laker	129
Fred Trueman	160
Brian Statham	161

ONE
S. F. Barnes
by Sir Neville Cardus

SYDNEY FRANCIS BARNES was born at Smethwick, Staffordshire, on April 19th 1876, and died near Cannock, Staffordshire on December 26th 1967. For forty-five years he played professional cricket, ranging from Test matches to Saturday games.

In his first-class career his bowling reaped for him 719 wickets, average 17.09. In all matches his figures, staggering credulity, were: 23,509 overs and 3 balls: 6,784 maidens: 51,890 runs: 6,229 wickets: average, 8.33. In Test matches (*v.* Australia and South Africa) his harvest was 189 wickets, average 16.43, taken in 27 engagements. Of these, 106 accounted for Australians, and 83 for South Africans. Of all the great cricketers who had to cope with Barnes's bowling, or who on the field of play could watch his attack at close quarters – Sir Jack Hobbs, A. C. MacLaren, Clem Hill, M. A. Noble, G. G. Macartney, Wilfred Rhodes, J. T. Tyldesley, to name a few – of all these, only one has hesitated to share their opinion that Barnes, more than any other bowler, had claims to be regarded the most difficult to master of all.

The exception was C. B. Fry who, not, of course, questioning the resources and powerful range of Barnes's arts, once told me that, of the two geniuses of spin and flight and variation of pace, he had found George Lohmann the more troublesome and persistent. George Lohmann, true, actually excelled the Test match bowling statistics of Barnes: 112 wickets at 10.75 each, taken in only eighteen games, fifteen *v.* South Africa.

Fry was, needless to say, qualified to discuss Barnes with some authority. In May, 1903, Fry playing for Sussex at Old Trafford *v.* Lancashire, in first on what *Wisden* described as a 'somewhat fiery wicket', scored 181, c. Eccles b. Brearley, and 20 not out. Ranjitsinhji, in the same innings, toyed with the Lancashire attack of Barnes, Brearley, Webb and Sharp, while conjuring a lithe 105. Barnes sent down 36 overs for 117 runs and the wickets of 'Ranji' and Newnham. That 1903 season was Barnes's last for Lancashire.

He disagreed with the Lancashire C.C. Committee, who declined to find him winter employment, or guarantee him a benefit match against Yorkshire. Barnes, in a period when the most renowned professional players were, so to say, housed in the servants' quarters of the pavilion, decided to confine himself mainly to

League cricket on Saturdays. His only two full seasons of first-class County cricket were with Lancashire in 1902 and 1903, when his performances as bowler were 82 wickets, average 21.43, in 1902; and 131 wickets, average 17.85, in 1903. But, as everybody knows who knows the first thing about cricket at all, A. C. MacLaren invited him to go to Australia with his England team of 1901–1902 – invited him on the strength of a single inspired stretch of bowling *v.* Leicestershire in 1901, 6 for 99; and of some experience of him in the nets.

All cricketing England, especially in the South, laughed at MacLaren's choice. Why, *Wisden* had remarked that Barnes could not bowl an off-break. And anyhow, who was this unknown league practioner; what would happen to his attack on the heartbreaking 'billiard-table' wickets of Australia, confronted by Trumper, Hill, Darling, Noble, Gregory, Duff and the rest? MacLaren's gamble – and he was sometimes a reckless speculator – 'came off' sensationally; alas, MacLaren's satisfaction had a bitter-sweet shortness of duration.

MacLaren's England XI won the first Test match by an innings and 124, at Sydney, in January 1901. Barnes wrecked Australia's first innings, 168 all out, in response to England's 464, Maclaren 116 and Barnes 5 for 65. In the second game of the rubber, though Australia won, Barnes's rewards were 6 for 42 and 7 for 121. Then, in the third Test match, at Adelaide, Barnes twisted his knee, the spikes of his boots penetrating the earth too tightly. This injury put him out of the match, after he had bowled only 7 overs for 21 runs and no wickets; what was worse for disillusioned MacLaren, it put Barnes out of the 1901–1902 Australian rubber for good (or ill).

Owing to this physical flaw, which recurred at times for subsequent seasons, he left the field at Lord's at the outset of the Gentlemen *v.* Players match of 1903. In the Gentlemen's second innings, MacLaren 168 not out, and Fry 232 not out, played Coronation cricket of unparalleled magnificence. The sweating professional colleague of Barnes, during this regal game, frankly did not take the most charitable view of affairs when Barnes departed from the scene, after turning his arm to the extent of a single over.

He always put a value on himself, once he had discovered his true bent. His career began inauspiciously, entirely without prophecy. He made spectral appearances for Warwickshire in 1895-1896, as a fast bowler pure and unsubtle; and in these seasons his record was without a hint of distinction: 86 overs, 226 runs, 3 wickets. In fact, when MacLaren decided to put his money on Barnes for Australia, Barnes's contributions to first-class cricket so far almost guaranteed bankruptcy: 13 wickets, 486 runs. Well may we echo the remark made by Leslie Duckworth, in his classic biography of Barnes: – 'One can imagine the sensation the choice for a Test match tour of a player with so undistinguished a record would cause today'.

I first saw him bowling for Lancashire at Old Trafford on the Coronation Day of 1902: the national holiday was kept, even though King Edward, suffering from appendicitis, couldn't be crowned. Old Trafford, flooded with sunshine from dawn to sunset, saw Lancashire demolish the Surrey attack. J. T. Tyldesley crashed 165 against them. Tom Richardson bowled for hours, swarthy and handsome, with a leonine moustache and black curly hair. He ran to bowl in long, beautiful strides, culminating in a glorious leap upward, as he swung over his right arm. Tom Richardson was Barnes's favourite bowler. He once said that he modelled his style on Richardson, and to his life's end has maintained that Richardson was the greatest bowler of them all – not excluding himself.

In this 'Coronation Day' game between Lancashire and Surrey, Barnes took 6 wickets for 39 in Surrey's first innings, then, after Lancashire had amassed more than 500, Barnes again threatened to annihilate the Southerners. But V. F. S. Crawford came to the wicket at the crisis; and a tall stranger we'd never heard of named Captain H. S. Bush stayed with him. Lancashire schoolboys, myself again, one of them, suffered frustration. Crawford drove nobly, getting as far as 90. What is more, he drove Barnes straight over the Stretford-end sight-screen for 6. In his octogenarian years. Barnes told me he had only *thrice* in his first-class career been hit for six, once at Old Trafford by V. F. S. Crawford; next, in another hemisphere, by V. F. S. Crawford's more famous brother J. N., playing for An Australian XI at Brisbane *v.* the immortal England team of 1911–1912; and, lastly, by Charles Macartney, at Lords, in the Triangular Tests of 1912.

Frankly, we Lancastrian schoolboys, though of course we revelled to see Barnes humbling Southern and all other alien batsmen, never really took him to heart, as we indeed did take to heart Johnny Tyldesley, Johnny Briggs, Albert Ward, Walter Brearley – yes, even in those distant departed summers we called our favourite cricketers by their first names; but not all of them. We would no more have referred to MacLaren as Archie than to W. G. as William Gilbert; MacLaren was known exclusively as A. C. MacLaren. Barnes had in our young eyes – and in the eyes of most mature batsmen of the day – an aloof 'lone wolf' appearance, six feet tall, a hatchet jaw, piercing, unsmiling eyes, and a lean and hungry look, hungry for wickets. During his only two seasons in the Lancashire XI, we could not think of him as one of our beloved Lancashire cricketers. Even Albert Ward, from Yorkshire, and Briggs from Nottinghamshire, somehow became Lancastrian by assimilation and adoption. Not so Barnes – he remained a man apart, a 'mercenary', so to say. I remember him as a player who most times seemed to isolate himself in the field; he wasn't 'given to chatter' at the fall of a wicket. He sent a chill wind of antagonism blowing over cricket fields everywhere. In our own time W. J. O'Reilly was called 'The Tiger', and was supposed to announce in his every motion as he bowled that he hated the sight of all batsmen. Compared with Barnes, O'Reilly was a fount of beneficence and geniality. Yet A. C. MacLaren vowed that no bowler who ever served under his captaincy was so easy to manage as Barnes. 'I would toss him the ball, let him set his own field – and that was that ...'

On a certain historical occasion, an England captain did not toss the ball to Barnes at the beginning of a match. Our narrative now comes to the wonderful tour of the England team in Australia, 1911-12. 'Plum' Warner, the appointed captain, fell ill and for the entire tour and rubber J. W. H. T. Douglas took over. He lost the toss in the first Test match (played at Sydney), and on a burning day led his men into the field. Douglas ran ahead and commandeered the new ball. (A new ball at the beginning of an innings and another every so-and-so runs had recently become legal procedure for the first time). Barnes said to a colleague, 'What's he taking the new ball for – is he opening with Mr Foster?' Frank Foster, fast left-arm, was obviously entitled to the new ball at one end of the wicket. 'Looks like it', replied Barnes's colleague, answering his question. And Douglas *did* open the England attack that day at Sydney, December 15th 1911. Australia compiled 447,

Trumper 113, and won by 146 runs. Barnes's analysis was: 35 overs: 5 maidens: 107 runs: 3 wickets and, 30 overs: 8 maidens: 72 runs: 1 wicket.

The next Test match of that rubber is now known as the match of Barnes's finest hour. This time Douglas tossed the new ball to Barnes, Australia having won the toss once more. It is as well known in cricket history, as in history proper the battles of Hastings and Waterloo are known, that at Melbourne, on December 30th 1912, Barnes demolished the strong first line of Australian batsmanship by overthrowing Bardsley, Kelleway, Hill and Armstrong, in five overs for one run only. At lunch Australia had somehow acquired 32 for 4; after an hour and ten minutes ruthless, smooth, rhythmic action, Barnes had bowled 9 overs: 6 maidens: 3 runs: for 4 wickets. After lunch, Hobbs caught Minnett off Barnes, whose figures now staggered Australia from Freemantle to Darwen: 11 overs: 7 maidens: 6 runs: 5 wickets. The astounding fact of this renowned piece of bowling is that Barnes was suffering from some dizziness, actually saying to his captain that he'd have to 'chuck it – I can hardly see the other end'. In this Australian first innings, Barnes's final figures were 23 overs: 9 maidens: 44 runs: 5 wickets; in Australia's second innings he had to be content with 3 for 96. But England won, as indeed England won all the remaining three games of the rubber. Barnes had let Douglas know, in no uncertain way, who had claim to share the new ball with Foster. At the rubber's close Barnes – incredibly! – was second in the Test match bowling lists to Foster – thus:

	O.	M.	R.	W.	Average
Foster	275.4	58	692	32	21.62
Barnes	297	64	778	34	22.88

In a talk with John Arlott, Barnes tried to recall the occasion and each ball he bowled on his miraculous morning at Melbourne. The pitch was full of runs. The first Australian batsman to go was Bardsley. The ball 'swung into him and hit his toe, then on to the wicket; he was a left-hander'. Then Clem Hill, another left-hander, 'I bowled him the same ball as the one which got Bardsley. He played it. Next I bowled him a leg-break – to a right-hander – one coming in to him. And he played *that*. Then I sent him one on his leg-stump, and it hit the off... Hill paid me a compliment; he said he'd never had such an over in his life...'

Years after the event, Clem Hill himself described to me the over Barnes delivered to him. 'I was in first wicket down, after Bardsley had gone for 0. I got four, probably from Frank Foster, but between him and Barnes there was precious little choice. On the whole, I wanted to get away from Barnes. I played three different balls. Three balls to play in a split second – a straight 'un, an inswinger and a break back! Then came along one which was straight half-way, not more than medium-pace. It swerved to my legs, perfect for tickling round the corner for a single. But the ruddy thing broke across after pitching, quick off the ground, and took my off-stump.'

Charles Macartney maintained that at Leeds, in July 1909, Barnes bowled Victor Trumper, in Australia's second innings, 'with the sort of ball a batsman sees when he's tight. I was in at the other end, so I *know*!' The remarkable fact is that, after the minatory first appearance in Test matches by Barnes in Australia, 1901–1902, and after a single appearance for England at Sheffield in the 1902 rubber, lost by England by 143 runs, Barnes did not play for England again until the 1907–1908 rubber in Australia. I have been unable to find out why, in 1902, Barnes was left out of the tragically decisive match at Old Trafford (engraved on the heart of poor Fred Tate, father of Maurice). In the preceding Test at Sheffield, Barnes had taken 6 for 49 in Australia's first innings, and one for 50 in the second. Barnes told me that at the agonising end of the Old Trafford game, which presented the 'Ashes' to Australia by 3 runs, he was sitting on the professionals' balcony in company with George Hirst, who also was not chosen to play. And sitting on the amateurs' balcony were C. B. Fry and G. L. Jessop, also among the rejected.

Barnes, believe it or not, was asked to play for England only at Sheffield in the 1902 rubber – cast out after taking 7 wickets for 99. Moreover, P. F. Warner, and Lord's, left him out of the England team which went to Australia in 1903–1904; also he was not called on at all to bowl for England in the rubber here in 1905. We may take it for granted that Barnes, over these seasons of his historic rejections, was ready to play for England, if invited. Round about 1902, *Wisden*, severely criticising Barnes as bowler, declared that he 'had no off-break'. Barnes, decades after, told Leslie Duckworth that the reason why he was not called on to join Warner's team is 'because they said I couldn't bowl an off-break'. Anyhow, after the team's names had been published to the world, Barnes, playing for Lancashire at Lord's, 'whipped one down just outside Mr Warner's off stump which broke in and knocked over his leg-stump'. How like the man, always ready to administer the rod of correction.

I reckon that it was during the years 1907 to 1912 that Barnes was bringing to technical control his greatest trick. I called it 'the Barnes ball' forty years ago – the ball pitching between leg and middle stumps and turning abruptly across to, *and near or on*, the off stump. Also, he added to this most dangerous of all the bowlers' weapons a *spin* swerve. I remember talking in the early 1920s to M. A. Noble, one of Australia's greatest batsmen-bowlers and captains. He told me that he obtained his out-swing by spin, and could, after the ball had pitched, cause it to break back from the off.

In his day, a new ball was available only at the beginning of an innings. Barnes admitted to Leslie Duckworth that he got the idea of the 'Barnes ball' from his close observation of Noble's bowling, during the 1901–1902 rubber. For years, Barnes privately practised the technique necessary to master this outswing which came back at the batsman. According to J. T. Tyldesley, Barnes did not command his 'trump card' while playing for Lancashire, between 1902 and 1903, but depended on length, off-spin and a direction which created the illusion that the ball was swinging away. As late as the Australian rubber *v.* England of 1907–1908, Barnes on occasion, when the wicket was unhelpful and two batsmen were solidly anchored, actually resorted to bowling round the wicket, aided and abetted by four short legs.

He was picked for the England team of the 1907–1908 rubber only at the last minute, owing to notable defections – Fry, R. E. Foster, Tyldesley, Hirst and other notables declined to make the trip for various reasons. A. O. Jones, the captain, was in charge of these players: F. L. Fane, K. L. Hutchings, R. A. Young, J. Hardstaff, (father of the gallant, latter-day 'young Joe'), C. Blythe, A. Fielder, J. N. Crawford, J. B. Hobbs (his first taste of Test cricket), E. G. Hayes, W. Rhodes, J. Humphries, L. Braund, S. F. Barnes and George Gunn – the last named genius was called in to replace A. O. Jones who fell ill. George himself was in Australia at the moment to ameliorate some chest complaint. With characteristic contrariness, George headed the England batting list: Test matches, 462 runs, average 51.33; all matches 831 runs, average 51.93. Barnes had to content himself with 24 wickets, at 26.08 runs each in Tests, 54 in all games, at 21.94. This rubber was lost by England by four Australian victories to one. All matches of this period, played in Australia, were fought to a finish – a procedure which, I think, should never have been changed. At the onset of every Test match in Australia, in those years, we could say, as the first ball was bowled – 'One team or the other is "for it". There is no escape – every ball bowled will be a nail in somebody's coffin'.

The memorable fact – often forgotten – of the 1907–1908 rubber was not Barnes's contributions (though, as we shall soon relate, he enjoyed one crowning hour), but the superb bowling of young Jack Crawford, at the age of twenty-one. In the five Test matches he took, on indestructible and, for batsmen, paradisal turf, hard and shining, 30 wickets, average 24.73. But the priceless point of this performance was the batsmen dismissed by Crawford: Trumper three times, Armstrong five, Macartney three, Noble three, Hill twice, S. E. Gregory twice, McAlister thrice, Hartigan twice. Incredibly, Jack Hobbs was not chosen for the first game of this rubber of 1907–1908, even though A. O. Jones, usually an 'in first' batsman, was in hospital. England's openers at Sydney on December 13th were F. L. Fane and R. A. Young, today resting secure in partial oblivion. England lost by two wickets. Barnes 1 for 74 and 2 for 63, including Trumper. The next match was England's only victory of the five encounters. And Barnes, *as batsman* was, at the crisis, the decisive factor. England, set to score 282 to win, lost the ninth wicket at 243. Barnes 38 not out, and Fielder of Kent, kept eyes on the ball. At the pinch Barnes recalled aeons afterwards, Armstrong bowled with all the fieldsmen except three on the leg-side. Nothing new under the sun.

Barnes, it may be mentioned here, was no novice with the bat. In club cricket of various sorts – and he changed colours and captains many times – he compiled his fifties. For Porthill, in 1910, he amassed 758 runs, including an innings of 129 not out, average 68.90. Next summer, for Staffordshire, when he took 104 wickets at 7 runs each, he had a match almost to himself *v.* Durham, in which he scored 136 and took 17 wickets for 83, nine in the first innings for 37. I seem to remember watching Barnes making a big score – maybe a century – at Old Trafford on a Whit-Monday for Lancashire Second XI v. Yorkshire Second XI. (Is it conceivable that the Lancashire County Committee even relegated Barnes to the reserve forces?) Possibly. He was left out of the Lancashire XI proper on one occasion because – the committee told him – the wicket was likely to take spin! What with *Wisden* and Warner thinking Barnes couldn't bowl an off-break, and what with the Lancashire pundits dropping him for a match to take place on a spinners' wicket, we are almost obliged to ask what manner of mysterious cricketer this Barnes was, in the beginning.

There was little enough to his family to influence or breed a cricketer, though his father played a little just for fun (did Barnes ever play just for fun? – a rhetorical question, of course). Barnes joined the local Smethwick team, third XI, when he was about 15. He received a few hours instruction from the club's coach – and that is all the coaching he absorbed in his life. He learned by experience, by trial and error. In one match, during his 'prentice days, he actually kept wicket – Mephisto a mere accessory of the attack! It's as though Authentic Mephisto had begun as a slave in the sulphur mines. Of all the great cricketers I have spoken to with any free and intimate exchange of views, Barnes was the most incrutable. He could not explain his own devices. To quote from the interview with John Arlott:

'Now, the legend is that even on perfect wickets you bowled a leg-break. What about this particular ball?'

'Well, I don't know; it came along with the others.'

'How did you bowl it?'

'For a fast ball, a fast-leg-break was exactly the same as bowling an off-break.'

'Did you spin it off the third finger?'

'Yes, every ball that I bowled I had to spin – fast, slow or medium.'

As illuminating as a dark lantern! It is, I gather from the evidence of a number of experts, including Mr Ian Peebles, at any rate clear that Barnes executed his leg-break without turning the wrist, an action which gives some notice to the batsman. Apparently Barnes manipulated the leg-turn mainly by leverage of the third finger – as most leg-spinners do, though most of them need to twist over the wrist. The off-spinner is controlled mainly by the first finger; at any rate, the first finger supplies the generating power. ('Ted' Wainwright, Yorkshire and England, observing that my own forefinger was on the small side, taught me to get the bias with the second). We can easily understand that Barnes had most batsmen guessing concerning the direction of his spin, if his wrist and palm of the hand were pointing down the wicket, with no hint of a wrist turn-over for the leg-break. But as Barnes himself would say 'I bowled the ball which circumstances and a batsman's particular style needed'. He confessed to me that he never bowled a 'googly'. The confession came from him after I had told him that Sir Donald Bradman once argued with me that W. J. O'Reilly was probably even a more resourceful bowler than Barnes, as he commanded all the tricks known to Barnes, flight, length, spin and so on, with the 'googly' thrown in. 'It's quite right,' Barnes admitted, 'I never bowled the "googly".' Then, after a pause, his eyes glinted, he added, 'I never needed it.'

Those born too late ever to see Barnes bowl might conceivably get some idea of his attack if they have watched Maurice Tate and Alec Bedser. I refer only to the actual bowling, not to the action directing and controlling it. Mentally mingle the best of Tate and Bedser: length, pace, swing, then add a tincture of O'Reilly, then, maybe some notion, some adumbration, will emerge or loom of Barnes in full spate. But, an important but – the delivery, the run to the crease and the physical motion of Tate and Bedser and O'Reilly were, in each case, arduous compared with the loose-limbed, flowing action of Barnes; a dozen strides, upright, apparently weightless, a gradual gathering of velocity, without jerk or obvious strain, then the rhythmical, not dramatic, upward leap.

'When I delivered the ball,' vowed Barnes, 'I wanted to look eight feet high. A batsman once said, "My god you look ten feet".' A. C. MacLaren, who fielded first slip to Barnes, assured me that Barnes seldom sent down a palpable loose one. 'If ever he looked scorable it was when giving curve through the air to his legbreak.'

In the heyday of Barnes, most batsmen, especially among the public-school products, played mostly off the front foot on good wickets. Even the Master, Sir Jack, qualified his prolific summers after 1919 by saying he'd made most of them off the back foot. In a game against Staffordshire, the 'original' Tyldesley, J. T. –

(brother of Ernest) – was captain, in his retirement from the first XI, of the Lancashire second string at Stafford, Barnes was quickly on the kill. Lancashire wickets fell; but J. T. saved the innings with 50 or thereabouts.

When he had scored twenty or so, he was missed at slip off Barnes, last ball of the over. Barnes stood still, gazing down the pitch, while the field changed position. His captain came to him: 'What's the matter?'

'Why' said Barnes, 'did Blank miss that catch?'

'Well – I suppose he just missed it,' was the surprised answer.

Again Barnes asked, 'Why did he miss that catch?'

'Oh, Barnes, how should I know? Anyhow, he missed it.'

'I'll tell you why he missed it,' persisted Barnes, 'he wasn't ready. What's more, Tyldesley won't play forward again all day.'

He was not tolerant of casual behaviour on the field or off. And his insight into a batsman's mind and technique was of terribly revealing depth. It was in another engagement between Lancashire and Staffordshire that a young Lancastrian (destined to bat for England) has his first experience of Barnes, when playing for the second XI. Lancashire won the toss, and the two openers walked to the middle, where Barnes was waiting, fingering the ball. The young novice, having noted that he was down in the order of going in number 7, put on his blazer and was about to leave the pavilion. 'Where are you going?' asked his skipper.

'I'd like to look at Barnes from behind his arm. I've never seen him before.'

'Go and put on your pads,' ordered his captain.

'But I'm not in until number seven,' pointed out the young novice.

'I know that,' said his skipper, 'all the same, get your pads on.' And the young aspirant returned to the players' dressing-room, where he joined four team-mates, all padded up. Each was 'wanted', himself included, within half an hour.

Barnes's performances in league and minor counties cricket make unprecedented reading and recording. He was the most peripatetic of professional players, going here and there, club to club, Rishton, Burnley, Church, Rochdale, Castleton Moor, Rawtenstall, Keighley, Smethwick, Porthill, Saltaire. But he remained faithful to Staffordshire from 1905 until the 1914 war; then, from 1924 to 1935, the year of his 62nd birthday. In this autumnal season of his career, his work was not heavy for his county – 90 overs, 255 runs, 9 wickets. In his sixtieth year he was fit and able enough to hold his own in the tight and technically and temperamentally challenging air of Lancashire League contests; for Rawtenstall, in 1932, his bowling figures were 440 overs, 819 runs, 113 wickets, average 7.25. Nearing sixty years, he was professional for Rochdale, with 114 wickets in the season of 1929, average 6.62.

It was, I fancy, during this 1929 summer that Patsy Hendren journeyed to Lancashire to play as professional in place of Castleton Moor's regular 'pro' who had damaged a hand at practice. It was permissible in those days for a League club to ring up Lord's for substitutes. As it happened, Middlesex had no match this particular Saturday, so Patsy packed his bag and travelled North. He arrived on the Castleton Moor ground early on Saturday morning to inspect the pitch. I'll try here to reproduce from memory Patsy's own words.

'A lovely day, and the groundsman was putting the finishing touches to the pitch. I pressed the turf. "Plenty of runs in it?" I said, "Yes, Sir, a beauty for a one-day match, though I say it myself".' Patsy again fondled the turf. ' "Yes, it *is* a beauty... By the way, it's a good game this afternoon?" "Aye, sir, a local Derby; Castleton Moor 'genst Rochdale. There'll be a full house." "Um – and I'm told that if the Pro does pretty well they send the collection round the crowd?" "Oh ay, sir – and there'll be a good 'un this match believe you me".'

Once more Patsy admired the pitch. ' "Yes, it's a beauty. And a good collection for fifty runs? By the way, who's the pro on the other side today?" "Sydney Barnes, sir". "Oh, gawd".' The drop of Patsy's mouth as he told this story is one of the recollections which will keep me silently laughing until life's close. 'We won the toss, and I managed to hang on. They didn't put the batsman's scores upon the board – just the total, fall of the wicket, and last man out; you know, 120–7–13. When a new batsman came in, he called down the pitch, "You're forty-nine". If I'd had any sense I'd have said to Barney, 50/50 shares in the collection. But I didn't, and next ball from him pitched on my leg stump and took the off, a brute of a ball.' 'But,' twinkled Patsy, 'I got my collection because I took 5 wickets for 50, and Barney was one of them.'

SIR NEVILLE CARDUS: *S. F. Barnes* 27

The zenith of Barnes occurred between the years 1911–1914. In three consecutive Test series he took no fewer than 122 wickets – 34 *v*. Australia in 1911–12; 39 at 10.35 in the Triangular games in England, 1912; and 49 at 10.93 each *v*. South Africa in 1913–14 (49 wickets, bear in mind, in four engagements!) – 122 wickets in 15 Tests, in one of which he didn't bowl because of rain at Manchester. In the wet English summer of 1912, when England, Australia and South Africa contended one against the other, his performances were these:

At Lord's *v*. Australia	0 for 74 (match washed out)
At the Oval *v*. Australia	5 for 30 and 0 for 18
At Lord's *v*. South Africa	5 for 25 and 6 for 85
At Leeds *v*. South Africa	6 for 52 and 4 for 63
At the Oval *v*. South Africa	5 for 28 and 8 for 29

At Lord's where for once in a blue moon, he failed to snatch a wicket, C. G. Macartney scored a battle-axed 99, when Australia went in facing England's 310 for 7 (declared). A team-mate of Macartney's that day – I think it was Bardsley – told me that as Australia's innings began and Macartney, in first wicket down, was putting on his pads, he said, looking out of the dressing-room window, down the wicket "Cripes, Charlie, Barney and Foster are at it again. Cripes, Barney's bringing 'em across from leg stump to off". Charlie said nothing, but when his turn came to go out to bat, which was pretty soon, he walked down the pavilion steps *livid with rage...*' He hit Barnes for six, as we well know. But Ian Peebles has provided the perfect coda or tail-piece to this momentous event. He asked Macartney, years after, what sort of bowler was Barnes. 'I'll tell you. At Lord's, in the Triangular set-up, I said to the boys in the dressing-room when I went out to bat, "I'll hit Barney for six". And, cripes, I had to wait till I was 64 before I could do it. That's the kind of marvellous bowler Barney was...'

In South Africa, 1913–1914, Test cricket was played on matting pitches. Naturally enough, the spin of Barnes became fantastically behavioured, gripping the resilient texture. It is fair to argue, on evidence provided by word of mouth from those who saw it all, and by statistics, that the bowling of Barnes in this South African rubber was the most unplayable, untouchable, ever known. Thrice an over Barnes's spin beat the bat and the three stumps. Strudwick behind the wicket, needed to be a spring-heeled Jack to give away in eight innings in which Barnes bowled, only seventy byes. Yet, in the face of the most difficult bowling extant, H. W. Taylor, for South Africa, batted eight times against Barnes, scoring 109, 8, 29, 40, 14, 70, 16, 93. But Barnes had his wicket five times. On the whole, I consider Taylor's batsmanship *v.* Barnes, on the mat in the South Africa rubber of 1913–1914, incredible to think of; it must count with the most skilful ever. Barnes did not play in the fifth game of this 1913–1914 rubber, because – independent yet and yet again, he disagreed with the 'management'. He related the affair to Mr Duckworth. The South African cricket authorities had promised Barnes they would do something to help him financially; he had taken his wife and son to South Africa for the benefit of their health. But they didn't do anything about it . . . So he turned obstinate.

Despite Barnes's figures in the South African rubber of 1913–1914, I can't, as evidence of his genius at its most versatile, set them above his figures *v.* Australia 1911–1912, where the opposition was stronger and, more important, where the wickets were more, much more, heavenly for batsmen. His victims in Australia 1911–1912, included Trumper, 4 times, Bardsley twice, Clem Hill 4 times, Armstrong 4, Kelleway twice, Ransford twice. In this rubber of 1911–1912, Hanson Carter, the Australian wicket-keeper, took part, scoring 13, 15, 29, 16, 8, 72, 6 n.o., 38, 11 and 23. He actually got 72 at Melbourne batting among the 'tail'. I recount these scores of Carter to lend point to a rich unselfconscious piece of humour on his part. In his retirement, we once discussed Barnes together. Without a blink, Carter said, 'I never had much difficulty dealing with Barnes . . .'

Round about the 1920s, J. W. Trumble, related to the more famous Hugh, wrote an article in *The Times*, maintaining with a quite forensic logic that the greatest bowler of all – to date – had been Spofforth. He admitted the skill of Barnes, but confidently voted Spofforth the superior of the two. Argument about circumstances usually ends in a beating of wind. But, surely, as we measure Spofforth and Barnes, we should emphasise that Spofforth bowled often on wickets rougher than any enjoyed by Barnes – even in club games.

My trump-card in the Spofforth-Barnes-Trumble dispute is this – Spofforth's most dangerous ball, as everybody agreed who saw him, was the off-break. As every schoolboy knows and as we have seen in the course of this chapter, the 'Barnes ball' spun the other way – from leg stump to off. Now there is a counter, an answer, to the off-break, which comes in to the bat. There is a stroke for the off-break – and on a good wicket even the 'modern' leg-cluster of fieldsmen is no guaranteed answer. There *is no reliable* stroke against the spinning away ball, unless it is a long-hop; and Barnes did not bowl a dozen in his career. The spinning-away ball, delivered at Barnes's pace, only subtly short of the length that impels a forward push, is nine times out of ten certain, by geometrical and ballistic law, to find the bat's edge. There is another point in favour of the claim for the ascendency of Barnes: his velocity off the pitch, off the beautifully-prepared wickets laid down in Australia in the 1900s onward, until 1938, laid down not for a few days but, apparently, for all time. The most marvellous fact of all the marvellous bowling conquests by Barnes is that it was in Australia, in the days of Australia's prolific harvest of runs, that the greatest of them were witnessed.

In 1928, the West Indians, on tour in England, agreed unanimously that Barnes was the most challenging bowler they encountered here in the season. A match between West Indies and Wales took place at Llandudno, July 25–27. I was there to see Barnes, aged 54 and some months, take 12 wickets – 7 for 51 and 5 for 67 – in 48 overs, confounding batsmen of the calibre of G. Challenor, C. A. Roach, St. Hill, R. K. Nunes, L. N. Constantine, E. A. Rae, C. R. Browne, O. C. Scott, all good players hard to stop scoring. Challenor, whom we might call the 'W. G.' of West Indies cricket, freely confessed that twice Barnes trapped him in the match, l.b.w. – 'I simply couldn't guess, as the ball floated fairly quick to the pitch, what it was going to do – leg or off spin'.

As late as 1929 and 1930, Barnes was to be seen in action at Lord's, in his 57th and 58th years, bowling for Wales *v.* the M.C.C. In the 1929 match, he phenomenally sent down 36 overs in M.C.C.'s first innings, and 39 in the second. His analyses in the two innings were:

36 overs 20 maidens 36 runs 3 wickets
39 overs 15 maidens 63 runs 4 wickets

In 1930, I saw him bowl for the last time, the game at Lord's *v*. Wales. He was like some visitation from history, for had I not seen him bowling for Lancashire more than three decades ago, in the reign of Queen Victoria? The man simply would not 'lie down'. At the age of 65 in 1938, he played for Bridgnorth, in Shropshire, and hauled in a hundred wickets – his season's energies worked out at some 300 overs for 126 wickets, average 6.94. We can easily imagine what destruction he wreaked in the Saturday games in leagues, this master of the greatest batsmen of the world, in different hemispheres, on perfect wickets.

I cannot here tell in detail of the marvels performed week by week, year by year for Porthill, Saltaire, Castleton Moor, Rochdale, Rawtenstall, etc., etc. For Porthill alone he took 893 wickets, average 5.28. He was professional for Porthill in the full noon of his power, from 1906 to 1914. It was after he had come back to England, conqueror of the Australian host at Melbourne 1912, that a young Lancashire lad answered an advertisement in *The Field*, wanting a professional bowler to play for an amateur side, on a tour in the midlands. He got the job, just one match, travelled alone, had lunch alone or with the other team's 'pro', who happened to be S. F. Barnes, very kindly to the nervous novice – off the field!

The novice batted number 11, and some twenty runs were needed to win. He put his bat to the ball; when Barnes bowled the boy was struck in the left rib, bruised by a red-hot missile exploding from the earth. No cricket ball every came from the pitch with the increase of velocity as cricket ball did when propelled from the fingers of Barnes. At any rate he created the impression of sudden and vicious acceleration. The novice, none the less, stayed in long enough to see the winning hit scored from the other end. Also, he received an extra five-bob with his fee of a guinea for the match. Barnes, no doubt, held the disgusted view that the timid tyro had not been batsman enough to get out to the ball which had harried even Victor Trumper.

He showed no mercy. He attacked a panic-stricken 'rabbit' as remorselessly as he attacked the Masters, one of whom, W. G. himself, he had encountered, for the first and last time, in the Gentlemen *v*. Players match at Kennington Oval in 1902 (there were two Gentlemen *v*. Players matches each season, those days) W. G. scored 82, c. Lockwood, b. Trott; and 7 c. Trott b. Lockwood. And Grace was then within a few days of his 54th birthday, so Barnes, who took 4 wickets in the match for 90 runs in 49 overs, was given a forcible example of the uses of longevity on the cricket field. Barnes related, in his dispassionate and accumulated years, that he appealed for a catch at the wicket against Grace, which was rejected; but when Grace got to Barnes's end he said, 'I played it, Barnes'. Clearly the 'Old Man' himself also achieved some dispassionate detachment, with the passing of time.

Barnes was a complete cricketer, not only a bowler possessed. Had he thought concentration on batsmanship worth while – necessarily worth *his* while – he could have developed to a dependable, straight-willowed, upright defender and maker of runs, scrupulously obeying first principles. Like Rhodes, he could in time have gone in first for England. In Minor Counties cricket his batting performances finally were as follows:

257 innings: 5,279 runs: highest score 150: average: 22.27 – and while I am reproducing these figures, I might press home still more astoundingly, the fact of Barnes's technical all-round mastery by quoting his bowling record for Staffordshire:

5,422 overs 3 balls: 11,651 runs: 1,437 wickets: average 8.10.

In his Test match experiences, 27 of them, only seven batsmen scored centuries against him – Clem Hill, three times; Trumper twice; Bardsley twice (in one and the same match – Kennington Oval, 1909); Duff, Armstrong, H. W. Taylor and Hartigan, the last four once each. Clem Hill, facing Barnes, also played one innings of 99, like Macartney. Indeed, Hill in three consecutive innings *v.* A. C. MacLaren's England XI in Australia 1901–1902, scored 99, 98 and 97, but after the making of Hill's 99 occurred the physical breakdown of Barnes.

I met Barnes in his mid-seventies at Trent Bridge in 1948, watching Lindwall attacking England's first innings. Hutton and Washbrook were immediately out. But Barnes, though admiring Lindwall, suddenly asked, 'Why does he send down a ball or two every over which batsmen needn't play? I never let 'em rest'. None the less, he agreed that Lindwall was first class. It was during this conversation between myself and Barnes that Wilfred Rhodes constantly interrupted, 'Who's bowlin' now?' and when we told him that 'Bill' Johnston had gone on, Wilfred's unseeing eyes gazed into the field, where forty-nine years ago he had first played for England. 'Is he still bowlin' over t' wicket?' 'Yes.' 'Why – he's a left-hander isn't he?' And repeatedly, Wilfred kept breaking in, 'Is he still bowlin' over t' wicket'. *Autre temps autre moeurs.* Besides, hadn't he seen Frank Foster, also quick left-hand, bowling over the wicket in Australia?

On another day, at Lord's, a long-hop was pulled deservedly round for four. Whereat a fieldsman was positioned where the ball had gone. 'Why has field been changed?' asked Barnes, 'does the bowler intend bowling another long-hop all day?' He gave the whole of himself, body and sharp intelligence, to the game; that is, on his inspired days. At times, but rarely, his fires seemed to burn without flame. Like Lockwood, he was given to moods which looked wilfully unproductive (but never for his league or Saturday club). As H. S. Altham wrote in his standard history on the game, Barnes was liable to vary 'between days of irresistible success and others when his temperament got the better of him'. On the whole, though, most players who at one time or other were his colleagues 'in the middle' have been emphatic that Barnes seldom spared himself.

'He was too ruddy bloodthirsty to slack,' said Clem Hill feelingly. 'The more I belted him,' vowed Charles Macartney, 'and I *did*, the more he made me sweat.' A. C. MacLaren, years ago, was positive on the point of Barnes' willingness to work. 'But he nearly broke my heart when his leg was strained in the third Test of the 1901–1902 rubber. He needed careful and tactful handling. He couldn't stand soft soap – neither could I. He was easily the most versatile and the most difficult of all bowlers I ever had to play.'

In his mellow last period, Barnes was beneficent, leading blind Wilfred Rhodes about the Test match grounds, thoughtful of his opinion, and many times generous. 'I'd have to be at my very best to keep this Bradman quiet.' 'I usually set the pace and bossed the show against batsmen, but Victor Trumper set his *own* pace. You couldn't dictate to him or to "Ranji".' He tremendously admired Maurice Tate; 'like me, he tries to get a wicket every ball, and is surprised if he doesn't'. 'A bowler should be ashamed – and *fined* – whenever he pitches short.'

His philosophy as cricketer is summed up in a letter he sent to the *Birmingham Post* in 1955 engraved in the beautiful copperplate script (engraved is the only apt word for it), which he used

SYDNEY FRANCIS BARNES 'His cricket was the man himself. It's hardly likely that the game will see the like of him again; a miracle in nature will be needed to produce his superior'

MAURICE TATE 'As a cricketer, he was a man of his time and it was a rich time . . . He will always be compared with Barnes, who came before, and Alec Bedser, who came after'

drafting documents for the Staffordshire County Council till the end of his nonagenarian life. He advocated a return to the 'old l.b.w. rule'. The 'present one' he insisted, 'favoured the inswinger, cramping a batsman's strokes. The going-away ball pitched on the wicket gets more men out with fewer balls. Make the batsman play at the pitch of the ball; he may get a few runs, but is more likely to get out.'

Barnes was always ready, tackling a great batsman on a true turf, to buy his wickets; he would 'feed' a favourite stroke, knowing very well that if such players as 'Ranji', Hayward, Hill, Trumper and the rest did not try to make strokes you would never get them out for hours. To bowl defensively is, for a bowler, a confession not only of weakness but of fear. Weakness and fear were not part of the constitution or nature of Barnes.

I suppose that Clem Hill did as well as most other batsmen, facing Barnes. In Test matches, with Barnes attacking him, his scores were: 46, 0, 15, 99, 18, 119, 87, 1, 16, 3, 5, 16, 7, 25 (run out), 12, 44, 46 (run out), 65, 4, 0, 0, 98, 17, 28, 20, 8. He was well qualified to describe the bowling of Barnes. 'I can't remember ever getting a really bad one from him. He kept you always on the alert – and' (with emphasis) *'he brought the best out of you.'* A splendid compliment; none could be better.

Another point worth consideration, as we make an estimate of the powers of Barnes, a point seldom if ever mentioned, is that, as he so rarely took part in first-class cricket, he was deprived of a constant foil bowling with him at the wicket's other end. Most famous bowlers have owed much to the fact of their having been perfectly 'paired' – for example, Lockwood and Richardson, Rhodes and Hirst, Gregory and Macdonald, Larwood and Voce, Tate and Gilligan, Tyson and Statham, Lindwall and Miller, Hall and Griffith, and so on. Only twice in his career did Barnes enjoy in first-class cricket a continuous and dangerous foil – J. N. Crawford and Frank Foster in the 1907–1908 and 1911–1912 Australian rubbers.

Only intermittently did he play for the Players *v.* the Gentlemen, at Lord's – in those days a great match of the year, a Test match in fact. In these games he bowled 312 overs for 687 runs and 45 wickets, average 15.26.

Even his most ardent admirers have sometimes deplored that Barnes was content to exercise his skill against less than equally skilful challengers. Some of his league performances are dazzling at one moment of consideration, ludicrous at the next – 150 wickets, in a Priestley Cup season, for 618 runs, average 4.11. Against Low Moor, 9 wickets in 23 balls, and not a run scored off him – some balls worthy of Trumper's or 'Ranji's' or anybody's steel! It's as though Yehudi Menuhin had been satisfied to play most times for the delectation of Palm Court. Barnes, in his early years as professional cricketer, was no doubt wise to think of his economic future; he saw about him too many old players reduced to straits of semi-poverty and no dignity. And in all Barnes's complex psychological make-up, dignity and independence stood forth. As he was coming to the end of his 88th year, I asked him one day at Lord's, 'What do you do in the winter'.

'Work,' he replied. He added that he was still writing legal documents for the Staffordshire County Council. 'How about transport on winter mornings?' I asked. 'I walk' was the sharp, rather indignant retort. His cricket was the man himself. It's hardly likely that the game will see the like of him again; a miracle in nature will be needed to produce his superior.

TWO

Maurice Tate
by A. A. Thomson

1

FOR ALL who played with him and watched him, the picture remains vivid and clear: a bulky figure ambling up the crease in half a dozen easy strides; an action that is dead sideways on to the batsman as the right arm sweeps over; the ball is delivered at seemingly medium pace and, the instant it lands, it shoots past the bat like a hissing snake. Tate has taken another wicket. My mathematically-minded friends assure me that this notion of a ball gathering speed off the pitch, like a boosted aero-engine, is completely illusory. It may be so, but when you consider the number of wickets Tate took in his first-class career, there must have been 2,783 victims of the same illusion, because to the end of their days they believed, or will believe, that the ball that got them out flew up off a length with all the malignity of the original serpent of Eden.

Sussex cricket, more than that of any other county, has been very much a family affair: from the Broadbridges to the Gilligans; from the Oakeses to the Parkses; from the Langridges to the Busses, Sussex has been populated by happy bands of brothers, with often a gifted nephew thrown in for good measure. Equally important, though less frequent, have been the fathers and sons. To sort out all the Lillywhites would almost require one of those Old Testament genealogies, where Mahaleel begat Enoch and Enoch begat Methusaleh, but with the Coxes and the Tates, the problem is simple, for George Senior began George Junior and Fred begat Maurice.

What is more, both family pairs were somebodies in their own right. George Cox Senior was a bowler who took nearly 2,000 wickets for Sussex, including a bag of 17 in one match not far off his fifty-third birthday, while George Junior, an unlucky man in the matter of England caps, was one of the half-dozen batsmen (or cover-points) of recent years whom I would have gone a long way to see.

Fred Tate was a sterling county cricketer, who captured over 1,300 wickets, including five for one against Kent. He is remembered, however, not as the useful performer he undoubtedly was, but as one on whom burdens were thrust too grievous to be borne;

who was, like Admiral Byng, the victim of almost universal execration and who was afterwards, though slowly, recognised as a plaything of fate.

The story of Fred's tragi-comic misadventures in the Old Trafford Test is mingled history and legend. I got it as a very small boy from my step-Uncle Walter, and to us in Yorkshire the crime was not the inclusion of Fred Tate but the exclusion of our idol, George Herbert Hirst. It is impossible to convey in a cynical and sophisticated age the depths of emotion stirred in 1902 by the selectors' folly. It was even written of the situation: 'Ministers of religion publicly prayed that heaven would open the eyes of these misguided men... When England lost by three runs, we felt this was the clearest instance of Divine retribution since the destruction of the Cities of the Plain...'

When we had finished chewing up the selectors, we started on Fred Tate, a good cricketer, a good father and an exemplary citizen. What, in Stanley Holloway's immortal words, had this poor burgher done? He had missed a catch on the leg boundary, a position in which his captain should never have placed him. Left in his usual place at slip, he would have been as safe as the next man. As it was, England's fiercely successful attack was checked, when Darling hit up a curling skyer in Fred's direction. It was one of those hideous moments when the fieldsman is alone in a friendless universe. (And they call cricket a team game.) The ball eddied and swirled and Tate, dancing in dervish agony, finally went the wrong way and lost it. This happened when Australia were 47 for four. Before the fifth wicket fell, 27 priceless runs had been added and, though Rhodes polished off the rest for another dozen, the initial damage was done.

Nor was this the worst. Set 124 to get to win, England struggled spasmodically and eventually there arose a sinister position, horribly similar to that in which England had been poised on the knife-edge of *nine wickets down and eight runs wanted* in the fatal Ashes match 20 years before. Poor Fred Tate, not necessarily any more in a state of chassis than poor Ted Peate, hit a rousing four and halved the deficit. Then – remember this happened in Manchester – a heavy shower drove the players off. When Tate returned to the torture, he launched another do-or-die swing, missed, and England had lost by three runs. Braund, the bowler off whom Tate had missed the convoluting catch, took him for a friendly glass and a word of consolation.

'Cheer up, Fred,' said Braund, 'it'll all be forgotten in a week or so.'

'It never will,' returned Tate gloomily and nothing could convince him. There is no record that he ever did cheer up, but the drama's first act ended with Fred's brave assertion that he had a seven-year-old kid at home who would make up for his lapses. That is the story. Truth or legend? Both, I think. What is to Fred's eternal credit is that, with all this burning ambition in his mind for his son's success, he never badgered the boy about it or made his life a misery, by hounding him on towards where his duty lay. More sensibly, he brought him up in an atmosphere in which cricket was the daily round, the common task. This indeed furnished all father and son needed to ask.

2

So our hero grew up and became a cricketer; at first, no more than a promising one. Born in 1895, he was only seventeen when he had his first trial for Sussex, in 1912. He played in one match, batted twice for an average of six, and bowled 14 overs, taking one wicket for 28. In the next two seasons he did nothing in particular and did it moderately well. By the time the first War broke out, he had played altogether in a dozen first-class games, scored less than 150 runs and taken 20 wickets, all told, with fairly harmless-looking off-breaks of slow-to-medium pace. His action was not unlike his father's, though they could not have been mistaken for each other. Maurice was then a tall, leggy lad, all knees and elbows, hardly as yet 'coupled up', and when in time he came to take over the paternal nickname of 'Chubby', he was as yet far from plump. He had taken his first trial at the nets two years before, but the only talent he had shown was the inherited ability to produce an off-break and it was this that got him his first professional engagement at a pound a week.

When he came back after his first-war service, he spent the rest of the winter working on a Sussex farm. Then came the hectic season of 1919 with its long hours and two-day matches, which virtually exhausted the average professional. But not Maurice

Tate, whose vigour found expression in cheerful batting, punctuated by honest thumping on the leg-side. For the first time he hit his 1,000 runs and this he, great bowler though he was to become, was to do a dozen times without a break.

By 1920 the county programme fell back into its pre-war three-day rhythm and nobody could dispute the ease with which he fitted into it. He was now stronger and sturdier; his batting was a firm part of the Sussex machine and his wicket-taking figures were improving. In the fine summer of 1921 he scored a massive double-century, gaining a reputation as the county's most promising young batsman for a long time. He took part with Bowley in a huge second-wicket stand of 385, a record even for the county of Fry and Ranji, and within 14 runs of the record for *any* county. We do not know what his father said about this, but a form-master's report might have read: Batting excellent; bowling, fair.

That appeared to point the way to his future, a by no means cheerless one, but in the following season, a vital change occurred. There are two versions of the happening. One, less dramatic, was that in an early Sussex *v.* Lancashire match, Ernest Tyldesley, a charming batsman and a chivalrous opponent, suggested to Tate that he should quicken his pace from slow-medium to quick-medium. The more lively version concerns a match at Eastbourne, where Hampshire were batting on a typical Saffrons wicket. Philip Mead was carrying out his routine war of attrition against the bowlers, blocking the dead-straight balls, treating those that shaved his bails with nonchalance, and tempting his victim into over-pitching or under-pitching, an instant example of crime and punishment. Tate grew exasperated, as well he might, for I remember an old northern bowler telling me: 'I'd rather have bowled at Hobbs or Hammond than Philip. With *them* there was at least a gleam of hope.' *Wisden* says that in the course of amassing 55,060 runs, Mead was actually dismissed 1,167 times. Nobody who ever bowled to him believes this for one instant.

Tate, stung by the sight of his best off-breaks mocked and murdered, released, partly in exasperation and partly by accident, a venomous ball which pitched on the off stump and, at a heightened speed before Mead could move over to cover it, spun wickedly across and took his leg-stick. The impossible had happened. For an ordinary off-spinner to penetrate Mead's defence was about as likely as piercing the armour-plate of a battleship with a pea-shooter; it was that lightning spurt, that uncanny acceleration that had done the trick and, if you had told the unbowlable Mead that it couldn't happen, he would have known better. It just had. Sussex lost this particular match, because of the later treachery of the Eastbourne pitch, but in that same Hampshire innings Tate took three more wickets, two of them with the same monstrous 'accelerator'. A new bowler, of the same name, had joined the Sussex attack.

So far, as almost always with Maurice Tate, both parts of the story are true, but an even more vital event had happened at the beginning of the season. A. E. R. Gilligan had been elected captain of Sussex. This was a happy augury for the county; for Tate, though he could not know it quite so early, it was an introduction to greatness.

From the moment of that devilish freak ball at Eastbourne, Gilligan was anxious to have it launched again. At the earliest opportunity Tate was hailed to the nets at Hove. A few 'unloaded' off-breaks came down and then – the projectile. Gilligan's middle stump not merely shot back but shot back through the net itself. Three times the faster ball came down, like a poison-pill disguised in a confection of conversation lozenges. The captain then demanded a straight over of 'the hard stuff' and three of the six balls spreadeagled his stumps.

In the next match at Hove against Essex, Tate took four for 25. And still the wonder grew, for in the game that followed, also at Hove, this time against Middlesex, the action was seen that we came to know and recognise: the ambling steps, the sideways turn and then – bingo. Before lunch he had disposed of Haig, Hearne, F. T. Mann, Twining and G. O. Allen and the enemy score at lunch was 26. Before Middlesex were all out for 125, he had taken another wicket, that of G. T. S. Stevens, the only batsman who had shown the slightest sign of coping. This happened on August 5th and though, oddly enough, Sussex also lost this match, nothing could detract from Tate's personal achievement.

Another game, later in the month, when Tate and his colleague Roberts shot out lordly Yorkshire, the eventual champions, for 42, showed him to be almost unplayable when at Hove the foggy, foggy dew was followed by strong sunshine. In the end Rhodes, with six for 13, was even more destructive, but, considering Yorkshire's batting power, Tate's capture of five for 20 had more intrinsic merit. By the end of the season he had doubled his 'takings', passed his 1,000 runs, and completed the first of his eight doubles.

Gratifying as individual success was, there was more in it than even this spectacular advance. He was serving a leader who was both generous and discerning and who remembered how often the most eminent fast bowlers had hunted in couples, notably McDonald and Gregory, who had crushed the best of England's batting the season before. For a time – for all too short a time, as it turned out – it was not so much Tate or Gilligan, as Tate *and* Gilligan.

3

At twenty-eight Tate was at the height of his physical powers; tall, muscular, by no means graceful in movement, but immensely strong in arms, chest and shoulders. He was now beginning a golden era of three seasons in which he became England's outstanding bowler. For three successive summers he performed his own special kind of double, taking 200 wickets and making 1,000 runs, and, dovetailed in between these, was a Test performance in Australia, the taking of 38 wickets in a rubber, a figure which had not been touched before and has only twice been beaten since, by Bedser in 1953 and Laker in 1956. His career figures of 2,783 wickets and nearly 22,000 runs were, heaven knows, enormously impressive, but there is something astonishing in the way the heart of his cricketing life is concentrated into his own personal golden age. In those three seasons and one tour, gloriously spent on the heights, he took 733 wickets and hit, with a certain amount of impatience, 4,381 runs. For a comparable harvest, you can think of only Grace in the 1870s and Woolley and Hammond in the later 1920s and all the time he was playing cricket, as so few have done, for sheer enjoyment. For him cricket was often funny and always fun.

It seems remarkable in 1923 that anyone who bore his county's heaviest bowling burdens should bat so zestfully, but the zest was all in character. He was gloriously fit and on top of his world.

He was a member of the ideal combination, Gilligan and Tate, the fiercest pair of pace bowlers in the country, but so much more than that. What an admirable captain Gilligan was! He could inspire by an example that needed little precept; an example that placed Sussex among the most attractive batting sides and made them without question the Championship's keenest fielding side. He was himself the best mid-off of the day; probably, with George Hirst, the best of any day.

At the top of his form Tate virtually ate up the opposition; against Essex he took eight for 37, seven of them clean bowled, in an innings held together by the obduracy of J. W. H. T. Douglas. Imagine the most exuberant bowler of the age pitted against its grimmest batsman, who held on for 42 not out, with hardly a peep out of anybody else. A battle for the gods. Against Nottinghamshire, second in the table that year and a tough batting side, Tate, with vigorous assistance from Gilligan, took thirteen for 68. George Gunn and Whysall started Notts's second innings with an excellent stand of 56 and then Tate demolished the rest of the innings, allowing not a soul to reach double figures. Alas, poor Glamorgan! Tate wrecked their first innings with a shattering assault of eight for 30; he then pitilessly battered their bowling for 76 in less than an hour, mostly in boundaries. He was in fact in such destructive mood that Gilligan, out of sheer compassion for the routed foe, did not give him the ball in the second innings, leaving somebody else to finish off Sussex's job.

With almost any other bowler it might have grown monotonous; seven for 26 against a Gloucestershire that contained Walter Hammond; four for 19 against Worcestershire; six for 28 against Northamptonshire; and then, in the North *v.* South and England *v.* the Rest games that were used as Test trials, seven for 51 (first two victims, Holmes and Sutcliffe) and five for 62, including A. W. Carr and A. P. F. Chapman. If six for 62 sounds a trifle ordinary it should be added as an unostentatious footnote that, after the Rest had laboured to 200 for four, Tate went on again after lunch and took five for none, ending the innings abruptly at 205. Monotonous, perhaps, for the procession of batsmen in full retreat, but for Maurice Tate it was literally fun and games. Nowadays we are always (wrongly, I hold) telling cricketers to be entertaining. Tate would not have understood such a demand. By being himself he was entertainment personified.

We might without disrespect or overstress compare Tate's 1924 with W. G. Grace's 1876; both, at least, were around the age of 28 and at the peak of their splendid physical resources, 'the young men rejoicing in their strength'. It was a South African summer and the visitors were a competent side, but they had reckoned without the firm of Tate and Gilligan. For the first half of the season nobody in Test or county cricket could cope with them. They were, until the Oval Gentlemen v. Players match, the deadliest pair of pace bowlers in the world.

First it was one, then it was the other; often, as in the dramatic first Test at Edgbaston, it was the two of them together. Tate started in May with five for 38 against Hampshire; six for 24 against Gloucestershire, and six for 50 against Warwickshire. The pair of them began flaming June with a big win over Middlesex at Lord's, where Tate took seven for 39 in the first innings and Gilligan eight for 25 in the second.

There was naturally no doubt that they would appear in the side picked for the first Test at Edgbaston, where Herbie Taylor, South Africa's most classical batsman but a fallible captain, won the toss and asked England to bat. His experiment was unsuccessful. Coming together at international level for the first time, England's greatest pair of opening batsmen, Hobbs and Sutcliffe, by their own blend of watchfulness and artistry, carried the side through whatever perils South Africa's captain had suspected in the wicket. By the time Woolley and Hendren came along, the going was easier and Kilner hit out briskly towards the end of the day. Next morning England's total rose brightly to 438 and, when South Africa went in, nobody expected the sky to fall. Metaphorically, it did. In three quarters of an hour, in twelve overs and three balls, Gilligan and Tate sent South Africa back for 30 runs, only 19 of which came from the bat. Taylor, with a valiant seven, was top scorer and, while Tate took four for 12, Gilligan's share was six for seven. Here was the most fearsome act of destruction perpetrated on a Test side, even more devastating than the feat of 22 years before when on the same ground Hirst and Rhodes had routed the Australians for 36. The astounding thing about South Africa's demolition was its achievement by a pair of opening bowlers on a pitch free from evil without assistance from Parkin, who, with Richard Tyldesley, had made short work of the same batsmen in their county match against Lancashire.

It would be easy to write off the South Africans as a mere bread-and-butter side; easy, but unjust, because they made a magnificent recovery in their second innings, almost forcing England, who had made them follow-on over 400 behind, to bat again. But, small score or big, one answer was the same. Once more Tate and Gilligan took the wickets. Parkin, Kilner, Fender and Woolley bowled 65 overs between them without reward.

England won the second Test at Lord's by the same margin, an innings and 18 runs. Tate and Gilligan again had excellent figures, though they were not so spectacular as before. What I remember best is the batting of Hobbs and Sutcliffe, who scored 268 for the first wicket – England declared at 531 for two – and I vividly recall over half a life-time the descriptive phrase of my then favourite correspondent: ... 'Hobbs and Sutcliffe, jaunty as peacocks in the evening sunlight...'

The third Test at Headingley saw another win for England and another penetrative performance by Tate who, 'with nothing in the pitch to assist him', took six first innings wickets for 42. Repeating their Edgbaston pattern, South Africa made a high-spirited recovery in their second innings, but without sufficient strength to stave off defeat. Tate, who shared the spoils with Richard Tyldesley, had so far captured 21 wickets in the first three Tests, which had already given England the rubber. The fourth Test was wrecked by rain before even one innings could be completed. Even so, Tate had time to take three of the four wickets that fell and in the fifth, also bedevilled by the weather, he was again England's most effective bowler with three for 64. Thus he ended his first series for England with a tally of 27 wickets at something less than 16 apiece.

But between the third and fourth Tests a cricketing tragedy had happened. In the Gentlemen *v.* Players game at the Oval in early July Gilligan was struck over the heart by a lifting ball from Pearson of Worcestershire. Tate, who had been bowling at the other end, moved with characteristic speed from slip to pick the victim up. The bruise was horrible and the doctor who saw it told the patient to rest. The patient's idea of rest was to go in at No. 10 in the Gentlemen's second innings and, with quite staggering brilliance, hit a century in under an hour and a half, a high proportion of it in boundaries. It was entertainment in excelsis, but it was tragedy, too.

Tate, and a good many Sussex followers, would have wished their captain a duck instead of that hectic hundred, because Arthur Gilligan, in a sense, never recovered from the blow and its sequel. A fine all-rounder and a deeply respected leader he was to remain until the day of his retirement, but never again was he to bear his due part in a havoc-wreaking combination, fit for a time to be named with Lockwood and Richardson or Lindwall and Miller. This, faithful supporters believed, was why Sussex, bonnie fighters though they were, did not carry off the Championship. They would undoubtedly have had every chance of running second.

With 205 wickets and 1,419 runs in his bag, Tate was one of the first, along with Hobbs, Sutcliffe and Gilligan, England's chosen captain, to be picked for the next winter's tour of Australia. It is a tour that has been depicted in vivid narrative by one of Australia's most powerful captains, M. A. Noble, under the title, *Gilligan's Men*. The Englishmen played finely together as a team – the mere presence of Gilligan ensured that – but it is equally certain that, as individuals, Sutcliffe for batting, and Tate for bowling, were Gilligan's leading men. From first to last Tate worked like a demon, almost at times to the limits of human endurance. England lost the rubber, but lost it heroically, fighting a strong Australian eleven and manifold misfortunes at the same time. Like F. R. Brown's team 26 years later, they lost by four matches to one, but many, not all in England, had the feeling, especially when Australia won the third Test by a mere eleven runs, that any slight run of fortune's wheel might have sent the result spinning the other way.

In the course of the tour Tate bowled well over 500 overs, three-fifths of them in Tests. To a bowler brought up on English turf, Australian wickets were iron-hard, and remember that each of his 525 overs had eight balls in it. Here it was that the summer's accident to Gilligan began to take its toll for, inspiring skipper and superb fieldsman though he was, he could not give Tate the contribution which had made them so formidable as a pair. Wisdom after the event is easy and it was obvious that some other fast-medium bowler should have been sent to share Tate's burdens. As it was, the best help he received came from Roy Kilner, one of Yorkshire's traditional slow left-handers, who took 17 Test wickets, as against Tate's 38. Everybody else, including

Gilligan, found their takings all too expensive.

Tate could hardly wait to be among the wickets, though he was not let rampaging loose upon the weaker sides. It was in the first State game against a strong New South Wales eleven that he launched his first salvo by taking seven – Macartney, Andrews, Taylor, Kippax, Gregory, Oldfield and Nothling – for 74. Then, in the first Test at Sydney, he carried England's bowling on his broad back. England's batting except for Hobbs and Sutcliffe in both innings, Hendren in the first and Woolley in the second, was frighteningly brittle, but Tate, in a match of massive scoring, decorated by six centuries, was masterfully consistent. The heat was, as Australians said, suitable to Satan; the Sydney wicket was like marble, but in the match he bowled 89 eight-ball overs and with every one of those 712 deliveries he meant to take a wicket. All the time he was suffering extreme pain from a toe-nail that was being forced back into the flesh by the regular impact of his boot on the hard ground. Twice during the first day he left the field, received an injection and returned, not only to take another wicket, but eventually to suffer more fearful pain.

Over 160,000 people watched the match and it seemed that the entire population of our island waited with baited breath for news of the progress of the game and the state of Tate's toe. The thing, you might say, magnified itself out of all proportion. I remember an article by Herbert Farjeon which began: 'The world at this moment does not know whether Tate's toe-nail is on or off...' I also recall feeling indignant that anybody should make a mockery of so sacred a subject. Ah, well, we are all sophisticates now, but it is hard to withold admiration from a display of naked fortitude in body and spirit. After all, he was not a grim Spartan, inured to silent suffering He was, on the contrary, a jolly extrovert, used to joking and laughter, and the effort of plugging away hour after sweating hour with more pain than reward meant a double strain upon one of his temperament. England lost by 195 runs on the seventh day, but Tate came out of the game with as much credit as any of its six centurions.

The rubber followed its course; the second Test followed the broad outlines of the first. Again Australia won the toss and scored hugely in easy conditions; again England, apart from Hobbs and Sutcliffe, batted feebly; again Tate bowled heroically and again England lost, though by a much smaller margin. Tate's six for 99, four of them clean bowled, was the finest piece of bowling in the match and, as his colleagues repeatedly said, it wasn't so much the wickets he hit as the number of times he missed the stumps by a whisker...

At Adelaide England lost the rubber, though they came within eleven runs of winning the game. This was the one match in which Tate bowled fewer overs than usual, because the state of the wicket was more encouraging to Kilner and Woolley, but he twice batted more relevantly than a number of the accredited batsmen. Back at Melbourne, the fourth Test was the only one in which Gilligan won the toss and England the match. For once their batting was both well balanced and attractive and Tate's bowling, five for 75 in Australia's second innings, was one of the major causes of victory, the last four wickets falling to him for 21 runs. Even in the unhappy fifth Test, in which England's batting crumbled like shortcakes before the new terror Grimmett, Tate batted more resolutely than anybody else and made top score in the wretched second innings. His bowling remained as vital as ever and the game's nine wickets brought his record for the rubber up to 38. That lightning lift off the pitch had never been sharper and Strudwick, England's wicket-keeper, confessed that he found it easier to stand back, which he would not have done to an ordinary medium-fast bowler.

If there was one thing that underlined what in his jolly malaprop way he called his *stannima*, it was the gusto with which he went thumping into 1925 without respite, hard on the heels of a strenuous winter. In those days nothing could tire or discourage him. Not only did he complete for the third time the specialised double of 200 wickets and 1,000 runs, which nobody had or has done before or since, though Albert Trott did it twice in 1899 and 1900; in 1925 he captured his largest total of wickets, 228, at the low cost of less than 15. This season marked a peak higher than the rest of the highest range. Only twice in the dozen seasons that remained to him was he to score more runs and never again was he to take so many wickets at such bargain prices.

Sussex did not enjoy as prosperous a season as their leading all-rounder, partly because their batting, as England's had been in Australia, was patchy, and partly because Gilligan, still suffering retrospectively from that damnable blow over the heart, was out of cricket half the summer. But Tate rode as high as ever, easily heading the county bowling and in the national averages second to Charlie Parker by point nought six of a run per wicket. He also hit two hearty hundreds, one of them, against Nottinghamshire, containing two sixes, a five, and a dozen fours. To take half the enemy wickets in an innings once, as he did against Leicestershire, Hampshire, Middlesex and Essex, not to mention Northamptonshire, Glamorgan and Gloucestershire, against whom he did it twice, became a mere matter of routine. In the Hove game against Glamorgan his plunder reached fourteen for 58 and in a Gloucestershire game which brought him thirteen for 102, he twice bowled Walter Hammond for a combined total of four.

The summer of 1926 found him in the England team which, after four drawn matches, defeated Australia at the Oval. It was a tightly-locked struggle, involving on England's part the shuffling of seventeen players, including two captains. Of the bowlers Tate was the only one to play in all five Tests and if his profit of thirteen wickets, the best though it was, sounds meagre, this must be set against the fact that not until the fifth Test did Australia play two completed innings; out of, in fact, a possible eight innings in the first four matches, only three were finished.

In the first innings of the Oval Test his three wickets for 40 played a vital part and his one-handed catch of Andrews at short-leg – I can still hear the almost simultaneous slap-slap of bat and palm – was one of four classic catches in Australia's second innings. With the bat he scored 56 for once out, which was more than Woolley or Hendren could manage, and I especially remember in England's second innings the slice-of-melon grin on his face as he tried vainly to persuade the canny Rhodes to take two runs when one was the more reasonable calculation. The Ashes had come back to England and those two had undoubtedly done their share towards winning them.

4

Every man has his four seasons: spring, summer, autumn and winter. With Tate his golden summer went on and on until it faded away into autumn as though it were loth to cease. His winter was short and bitter, but as yet it was far away. In 1926, besides his Test successes, he achieved another double. Frequently going in first, he finished second to Duleepsinhji in the Sussex batting and, in regular fashion, headed the county's bowling. Again he took almost automatically half of Kent's, Surrey's and Gloucestershire's wickets and staged a terrific performance in the Whitsuntide match against Middlesex at Lord's, dismissing nine for 71, three of them subscribing to a hat-trick.

So the seasons passed. In 1927 he set up his highest batting aggregate, which was 1,713, including four centuries, three of them in a row and one of them completed well before lunch. His wickets numbered 147, the same as in the season before. He also achieved his sixth double and a gem of bowling, even for him, was his six for 28, nine for 49 in the match, against Lancashire at Eastbourne. The undoubted fact about 1928 was that it confirmed Tate's position as England's finest bowler; his toll of wickets rose to 165 in a batsman's season and his runs, enriched by three centuries, came close to 1,500. He was one of the first to be picked for A. P. F. Chapman's team to visit Australia in 1928–29.

Chapman's side has been reckoned, by Sir Pelham Warner and others, as the best equipped ever to be sent from England to Australia. Without question their batting strength was prodigious and, if their bowling looked on paper a little less imposing, its quality was 24-carat. The wickets taken were shared fairly equally between Geary, White, Larwood and Tate and though, in this season of high-powered batsmen, bowling averages were bound to suffer, Tate was the one bowler the Australians truly feared. He did not get the fierce lift that had brought him his harvest four years before and his chronic habit of missing the stumps by a fraction of an inch continued to beset him. Nevertheless, he bowled like his own indomitable self. In the vital third Test at Melbourne, when Australia in the suffocating heat looked like tiring out England's attack, Tate was put on to keep down the scoring and bowled like a man possessed. Over after over he gripped the batsmen in a vice that made runs almost impossible. Nothing contributed more firmly and clearly to England's victory than this daemonic bowling.

Seasons come and seasons go but Tests go on for ever. The visiting South Africans of 1929 were a young and attractive, but hardly powerful, side and, while they made some handsome totals, they were not likely to dismiss a strong England eleven ten times.

England won the two Tests that were finished, mainly through the bowling of Freeman. Tate played in only three of the five, missing the last two because of injury, but he took more wickets than anyone except Freeman and, just for fun, hit an honest extrovert's hundred at Lord's.

He went on, with only one break, taking his 100 wickets a season until 1935, but 1929 had seen the last of his doubles. The season that followed was not an easy summer for him, if only because it was the season of Bradman's first invasion of our shores, after which life for bowlers could never be the same again. Australia took back the Ashes of which Chapmen's men had robbed them, and so comprehensive was their power that it was hard to conceive of any force that could have stopped them. No England bowler had an average of less than 33, but Tate's effort stood out like a lighthouse. The first game at Trent Bridge was well won by England and nobody was entitled to higher credit than Tate, not only for his match figures of 6 for 89, but for the ferocious breakback which disconcerted Bradman almost as much as the 'perfect' ball from Bedser which bowled him 16 years later.

No English bowler had a look-in in the mammoth-scoring second Test at Lord's, but at Headingley, scene of Bradman's fantastic 334, Tate battled through 39 overs to take five wickets, including Bradman's, for 104. He was caned as cruelly as any of the other victims at the Oval, but he took 15 wickets in the rubber and the best friends of Hammond and Larwood would have hated to remind them of their averages of 60 and 73. At least he had a field day when, on his county's behalf, he shook the Australians at Hove by shifting Ponsford, Jackson, McCabe, Victor Richardson, Fairfax and àBeckct before more than 18 runs could be scored off him.

The 1930-31 tour of South Africa was not an unqualified success, as the only completed Test was lost by 28 runs. Yet Tate, who started with 5 for 18 in his first provincial game, went on to head the averages both in Tests and for the tour as a whole.

A considerably improved Sussex rose to the fourth championship place in 1931 and thoughtful observers attributed this success chiefly to the work of one batsman and one bowler. The batsman was K. S. Duleepsinhji, nephew of the fabled Ranji, a young man of sincere and charming character and a batsman of elegant talents. The bowler was Maurice Tate, 36 years old and the taker of 141 wickets, 111 of them for Sussex. Picked in only one of the three Tests against New Zealand, he took four for 37, which gave him an average more striking than any other bowler's and, if anybody thought his first class days were over, he could always produce a 10 for 88, a 6 for 48, a 5 for 46, a 6 for 50, a 12 for 58, a 5 for 24 and, as we might reasonably add, so on and so on...

Sussex in 1932 had her most opulent season for thirty years. Yorkshire won the Championship in the end but Sussex, who lost only one match, ran them close all the way and generally played more fascinating cricket. Duleepsinhji hit five centuries and had an average of 52; Tate bowled 1,400 overs and took 160 wickets. There was hardly a match in which he did not average eight captures and against Middlesex at Lord's he had what he called a 'flippin' Bank Holiday', knocking down Middlesex wickets as though they were coconuts on Hampstead Heath. His total booty was 13 for 58. As he would have said himself: 'Some coconuts!' There would have been a public outcry if he had not been included in Jardine's 1932–33 team that went to Australia and won the Ashes.

He was unlucky from its start, because his journey was delayed by a kind of nervous illness and when he reached Australia, he found that he was cast for the part of Cinderella rather than his favourite rôle of Demon King. The tour rolled on its controversial way and Jardine had his own plan of attack, which did not include Tate. Nevertheless, in the first match after his arrival he got rid at moderate cost of New South Wales's first four men, one of whom was Bradman. Playing in only five first class matches, he gave of his best, finishing with better bowling figures than Voce or Bowes and hitting 94 not out, mostly in fours, in an exciting drawn game against Victoria. A disappointing tour, but at least he could not be blamed for the scars that it left.

Because in 1933 he failed for the first time in a dozen years to take his regulation 100 wickets, it was no serious sign of the onset of old age. After all, he had missed the hundred by only one and, though sensational performances were rarer, he did not fail to rub salt into the wounds of some of his old victims: Somerset, 5 for 13 (9 for 50 in the match); Surrey, 5 for 45, including Hobbs for a duck; Kent, 5 for 28; Glamorgan, 2 for 36, and Lancashire, 5 for 38. True, Sussex were that year a buoyant side, who twice beat the champions, and in James Langridge, Wensley and Jim Cornford there were new bowling powers in the land.

For the third time running Sussex in 1934 came second, pushing Lancashire, the champions, extremely hard. On Bowley's retirement, Tate was tried at his old position as opening bat, but an ideal opening pair came together in Jim Parks and John Langridge and Tate had to 'take it out' in bowling, which he did by capturing 142 wickets at an average of under 20. It was his last big bag. At any rate he gave some food for thought to those who shook their heads over his reputation as a bit of an irresponsible. When, as senior professional, he was called on to act as deputy captain he showed both seriousness and intelligence.

His fortieth birthday came in 1935, a season in which Sussex dropped five places in the table, and he took his 100 wickets for the last time. It seemed that age could not wither nor custom stale a bowler whose custom was to take 5 for 30, as against Worcestershire, 9 for 49 (Nottinghamshire), 6 for 26 and 5 for 23 (Essex) and 5 for 9 against Gloucestershire, his inevitable whipping boys. How was that, he might have asked, for *stannima* at forty? His final honour was a recall after four years to Test status against South Africa at Old Trafford, where he played a fierce little innings of 34, almost all in boundaries. He bowled neither badly nor well, taking 2 for 67. His victims were Cameron, the hardest of all South African hitters, and Bell, a similar kind of bowler to himself.

A. J. Bell, l.b.w. b. Tate 1

It was his last international achievement.

Sussex were full of trouble in 1936, falling with a severe bump to fourteenth place and Tate's 78 wickets at a cost of 22 runs each formed one of the compensations of an impoverished county season. With 743 runs and those 78 wickets he came as near to the double as many estimable cricketers ever achieve in their estimable careers. Committee members would remember his age, but they were, or should have been, inclined to forget it when they saw him demolish Hampshire at Hastings with a shattering 7 for 19. If this was but a flash of his old self in this sad year of his decline, there were other flashes that were positively blinding. Perhaps they did not, more's the pity, see his 6 for 57 at the Oval,

6 for 48 at Lord's, 5 for 48 at Ilford and, in a tight battle at Bradford, where battles tend to be tight, 5 for 33. The unlucky five were Mitchell, Yardley, Sellers, Wood and Ellis Robinson and I call them unlucky, because, as *Wisden* said, Tate disconcerted them by *his pace off the ground and his swerve*... After all, at any age, that was the real Tate... If in the season he hit 20 sixes, that was perhaps neither here nor there.

In the *Wisden* covering the 1937 season appeared two sentences which were masterly even by *Wisden*'s admirable standard of understatement. The first was: 'Tate made only infrequent appearances and at the end of the season Sussex announced that his agreement would not be renewed.' This was true, but it was about as near the whole truth as if Cromwell had announced that, as from February 1st 1649, King Charles would no longer require ruffs or plumed hats. In his infrequent appearances Tate took 46 wickets and his best figures, (apart from 4 for 51 against Warwickshire and 4 for 61 against Kent) were 5 for 43 (in the match) against Middlesex at Lord's, where he always pulled something out of the hat.

On August 3rd he was called to the committee room at Hove and told that from the end of the season Sussex would no longer require his services. Now there are two sides to every question, though the sides are seldom equal. 'Evil is wrought by want of thought,' said the old Victorian poet, 'and not by want for heart.' For 'thought' read imagination. The want of imagination in the manner of Tate's dismissal was stunning. People who slap paint on canvas or scribble words on paper are reckoned to be sensitive souls and some care is taken not to lacerate their feelings. For the feelings of Maurice Tate, an artist of high quality in a medium which in character and spirit is part of England, no such consideration was shown. It could be, and was, not unreasonably argued that he was the victim, not of ungrateful employers, but of the facts of life; that even the richest gifts fade and that the bravest cannot soldier on for ever. All this is true enough, but to Tate, a laughing philosopher without a touch of stoicism, it was as though he had been told: 'Well done, thou good a faithful servant; now go and jump of Brighton West Pier.'

He played in the remaining matches of the county programme. His last game was against Surrey; his last performance, not a bad one, considering Surrey's batting strength, was 4 for 116; and his last victim, clean bowled, was Alf Gover, a genial soul and a kindred spirit.

To quote *Wisden*'s second understatement: *Thus a great figure disappeared from the game.* In his remaining quarter of a century he did some valuable coaching and presided as friendly host at more than one Sussex inn. In 1949 under the presidency of the Duke of Edinburgh he was one of the 26 retired professional cricketers chosen as honorary life members of M.C.C. The election was restricted to 'the really great' and he must have grinned his quarter-melon grin over that. Though the last man in England to be rancorous, the hurt of his brusque dismissal stayed with him a long time. But not of course to the end. On his sixty-first birthday he accepted an invitation to umpire in the Australians' opening match against the Duke of Norfolk's Eleven at Arundel. He was in rare form and the long white coat and the jolly jokes about its being too small for him were stretched to the utmost. Three weeks later at his inn in Wadhurst he died suddenly.

5

Thus a great figure disappeared. As a cricketer, he was a man of his time and it was a rich time. It was the time when an English batting order could run: Hobbs, Sutcliffe, Hammond, Jardine, Leyland, Chapman... He bowled, often on billiard-table pitches, against Bardsley, Macartney, Ponsford, Woodfull, Bradman, H. W. Taylor and Catterall. In an era of batsmen he was one of the few bowlers who denied them complete mastery.

He will always be compared with Barnes, who came before, and Alec Bedser, who came after. They fall naturally into a trinity of high-powered fast-medium bowlers, easily the finest of their kind, and, strictly so far as batsmen were concerned, an unholy trinity. Each of the three has his admirers in and outside his own generation. The sweep of history, after we have gone, may put Barnes first, if only for the tremendous scope of his career. Bedser, with his 236 Test wickets, his brave battles with Bradman in 1946–47 and 1948, and his wonderful bag of 39 in 1953, will remain the man who restored the hopes of England's bowling after the war. But any comparison is a tricky business and, as always, there are too many imponderables.

56   *Cricket: The Great Bowlers*

Do figures help? Again the imponderables get in the way.

	Career Wickets	*Test Wickets*
Barnes	719 at 17.09	189 at 16.43
Tate	2,783 at 18.16	155 at 26.13
Bedser	1,924 at 20.41	236 at 24.89

For Tate there will always be a place in the affection of warm hearts and the intelligent appreciation of cool heads. He bowled against famous batsmen over a period when it was the universal pride of groundsmen to make life for the batsman one grand sweet song. Flip through your *Wisdens* from 1923 to 1936 and note how often you will light on the phrase, introducing some fantastic feat: 'Tate, with no apparent assistance from the pitch...'

If the three are to be measured on points, as at a show, I could not claim to be a competent judge, except to say that each was supreme in his era and that now abide these three...

What was the secret of Tate's technique? The secret was that he had no technique. If he told you he had, and explained it with a wealth of 'sesquippledan verbojuice' he would be pulling your leg. The fact is that, granted his vital change to the faster ball, he was a natural bowler in that he did not consciously, still less self-consciously, work out a scientific bowling policy. As he came up to the swing, he leant back on his right leg with his left arm stretched out in front. As the right arm came smoothly over, the full weight of his heavy shoulders was behind it. He used the seam in a way in which no bowler had done before and many without much success have attempted since. Ian Peebles says that he placed the ball with the seam between, and parallel to, his first two fingers, and let fly. It was that *let fly* that was characteristic and wholly natural.

Those who played closely with him appreciated him most. Hendren believed that he made the batsman play five balls out of six; Strudwick, who had more reason than most to know, called him the best of all the *length* bowlers, in the class of Barnes and Frank Foster, and S. C. Griffith, secretary of M.C.C., a former Sussex captain and a thoughtful student of the game, thinks that if modern field placing had been in vogue in Tate's heyday, he would have taken hundreds more wickets. Shots that then went harmlessly down the legside would have been short-leg catches today. Let C. B. Fry have the last word: 'He could make the ball swing away very late outside the off-stump, and even the best batsmen were often beaten by him. He could make the ball rear off the pitch like a snake striking...'

M. A. Noble described him as a shock-merchant. 'He indulges in a series of shock-delivering periods which invariably prove fatal to several batsmen. The ball... gets up quickly and venomously when bowled a good length – Tate always bowls a good length – and is a great source of danger to the batsman, especially in the opening stages of his innings...'

Noble has a charming way of criticising the bowler who was, at least until the advent of Mr Trueman, cricket's leading extrovert. 'He is a little lacking in self-control when he nearly bowls a man...' But this was all part of Tate's nature, part of his fun. He was nearly always nearly bowling his man and it would have been a miracle if he had not appealed to Eternal Justice by his wealth of word and gesture, when the frequency of his near-misses made Eternal Justice seem eternally unjust.

He liked to laugh, he liked to joke, he liked to talk all the time, and he would convert his observations to umpires and batsmen into resonant Chinese whispers by cupping a huge hand over his mouth. If there was no one near to talk to he would talk to himself in what he called a 'taty-taty'. He had a way of subjecting longer words to assault and battery more reminiscent of Mr Polly than of Mrs Malaprop. To him rude remarks were not opprobrious, but *opprolobus*, which is a better word, anyhow.

Once in Australia, after two ear-splitting appeals for leg-before, he strode down the wicket and addressed an apparently 'opprolobus' observation to the batsman. There were newspaper stories, which grew and grew, suggesting that Tate had been guilty of some monstrous abuse. Taxed by his conscientious captain to repeat the terrible objurgation, he strove hard to remember and then recollection dawned.

'Ah, yes,' he replied. 'What I said was: " 'ot, ain't it?" '

He was without question a man of his time, even if there were few in his time who were like him. He had visited, and made friends in, cities all over the world, but never ceased to be an English countryman; his humours resembled the humours of the rustics in an immortal wood near Athens, than which there can be nothing more English. More exactly, he was, I think, a link, perhaps the last, with the cricketers, the countrymen of the real old England. Could he, by some touch of the old country magic, have suddenly been transported to Broad Halfpenny Down to play for All England against the Hambledon men, nobody would have called him stranger. He could have bowled at Silver Billy Beldham and gestured in amazement when he failed to shift craggy old Tom Walker. He could have watched Brett's 'tremendous' bowling or picked up a tip or two from David Harris, who, after all, was father of Tate's kind of bowling, because he could make the ball leap devilishly from the pitch. 'It was but a touch,' said Nyren, 'and it was up again.' Tate's bowling precisely.

I can see Tate among the 'brown-faced farmers' and 'anointed clod-stumpers'; I can see him chatting with John Small, who was a fiddler; argufying with Tom Walker of the scrag-of-mutton frame and spidery legs and joking with Noah Mann, the laughing, eccentric character who, of all the Hambledon men, was most like him. There, drinking a mug of John Bull punch, at sixpence a bottle, he would be at home for, 'unadulterated rustics' though they were, not a man among them was more richly rustic than he.

When on a pearly summer morning at Hove the sea-fret comes rolling up across the ground, it is whispered that the ghost of Maurice Tate walks and wickets fall to the Sussex bowlers, good men all, though not so good as their famed predecessor. Wickets fall, I say and I have seen them, but not so regularly or so inevitably as when those long fingers curled round the ball till it looked like a pea in his hand and when, as he let fly, it came up off a length like a hissing snake.

It must tax all the powers of the Occult to manufacture a ghost of that solid, earthly chunk of masculinity, but, as the sea-fret delicately sways and swirls, fancy can at least picture in one whorl the vague outline of a laughing face, a bulky figure and two feet, none the smaller for being spectral. As another wicket falls, old gentlemen in the pavilion nod sagely.

'Ah, yes, there he is; his ghost walks...' They will recall him in his prime and, though not always agreeing on what was his most prodigious exploit, they are all agreed on one thing:

His heart was as big as his boots and his boots were enormous.

THREE

Harold Larwood
by Bill Bowes

1

THERE ARE certain experiences I believe every sportsman should know. He should see racing at Royal Ascot, a soccer cup final at Wembley, tennis at Wimbledon, a rugger international at Twickenham or a game between any of the Home Unions and England. If he is lucky enough to travel, the Olympics; baseball in America; a R.L. Test match in Sydney; and an Australian Rules final at Melbourne. A Test match at cricket on that same ground, and of course, a 'must' for everyone – a Test match at Lord's when the teams are evenly matched and the 'House Full' notices are posted. Some of these experiences I still hope to get, most of them I have had, and they will never be forgotten. With ideal conditions and perfect weather these occasions leave a memory to be cherished for life. They bring a remembered glow of satisfaction.

They are great sporting occasions in a general sense but, for every type of sportsman, other occasions in his own game are equally important. As a so-called cricket expert, that is, as a player from the late 1920s until 1947 and, from then on, a professional critic watching cricket every day of the summer, and every day of the Tests in England, I believe I have been lucky. As a result of the advanced techniques in batting and bowling which came with the improvement in pitches at the turn of the century (The Golden Age of Cricket) I believe I have seen – apart from Dr W. G. Grace for very obvious reasons – all the greatest players in the game's history. I played with and against the five great cricketing Knights: Sir Donald Bradman who was the best batsman of all time, Sir Jack Hobbs and Sir Leonard Hutton who were the best batsmen of England; Sir Learie Constantine (now being challenged by Gary Sobers as the best all-rounder to come from the Caribbean), and Sir Frank Worrell, the man of quiet strength and charm, who harnessed the exuberance and enthusiasm of the West Indies cricketers and put them on the road to being world champions.

I played with and against the three best equipped bowlers of all time, bowlers who could bowl everything, Barnes, O'Reilly and Appleyard; my standard for the off-spin bowler derives from

Clay, Goddard and Laker; and surely it would be accepted as fact that Rhodes and Verity were at the top of their profession as slow left-handers.

Even as I have mentioned these names, memories have come flooding back. Hobbs has steered me effortlessly to the fine leg boundary for four and stroked me through the covers just hard enough to beat the fieldsman to the boundary; Bradman has square cut and pulled with powerful viciousness. Hutton has played again that delightful delayed drive with bat going in the direction of cover point and the ball streaking to the third-man boundary.

The memory of Constantine following through after bowling to Woolley in a Test at Lord's – diving headlong up the pitch to get his hand to a defensive push forward but with his momentum knocking the ball forward again so that ball and outstretched fieldsman came to rest at the feet of the batsman while the packed thousands stood and roared their appreciation – was an occasion I lived again. This was followed by Verity's all ten wickets at Leeds, against Notts and Laker's all ten against Australia at Manchester.

But of all the memories the one I cherish most is that of Harold Larwood, 'Lol' Larwood of Nottinghamshire, to my mind the world's best and fastest bowler of all time. He was only a slip of a man, 5 feet $7\frac{1}{2}$ inches tall and weighing less than 11 stone, but he had muscles of coiled steel, hardened by work at the coal face as a miner, and one of the loveliest actions possible to imagine.

He measured out a 26-pace run, but he bowled off the fourteenth pace. His acceleration when he moved in to bowl was smooth and menacing. On the hard grounds of Australia his feet could be heard beating a quickening tattoo. He was moving so fast in his final stride he had a 'drag' of 32 inches but he started so far behind the bowling crease he seldom had trouble with a no-ball.

When his left foot hit the ground, there was a slide of a couple of inches but all these things seemed allowed for. It was the perfect action, and the perfection continued into the delivery itself. He had longish arms, the left shoulder pointed in the direction the ball was intended to go and the shoulder got to the fullest height possible before it started to swing downwards and outwards, so that maximum power of the body swing and shoulders came in, with perfect timing, to join the swing of the right arm flashing round with the ball in hand as if fastened to the rim of a wheel.

With such an action Larwood could not fail to have all the attributes needed for fast bowling. There was control besides speed, a deadly accuracy so fine that he could bowl down the line of the off stump or leg stump at will. He did not swing the ball, that is in terms of movement through the air, but, hitting the pitch with the seam upright he many times made the ball move towards the slips after pitching and he could move the new ball 'in' at the batsman in a manner that was obvious even to spectators – as much as four to six inches at times from the pitch to the stumps.

The nearest approach I have seen to the Larwood action was that used by Australian Ray Lindwall after the second world war.

By half-closing the eyes and watching Lindwall it was easy to think here was Larwood again and I was delighted on one occasion when, at Trent Bridge, a Nottinghamshire spectator accused the Australian of 'copying' Larwood. The spectator had intended his observation to be sarcastic but Lindwall squashed him in a second when he asked, so very earnestly, 'And why shouldn't I copy the master?'

Lindwall had seen Larwood bowl when he was a schoolboy and Larwood was a member of D. R. Jardine's 1932–33 tour to Australia. It was an unfortunate tour. It produced the greatest controversy of all sporting occasions, a type of bowling called 'Bodyline', ill-feeling between the two countries, an alleged feud between Bradman and Larwood, and led to legislation and changes in the laws of cricket. Larwood is remembered for his part in this controversy rather than as a great fast bowler – and I want to claim him the best of all time.

2

Since cricket was first played the question as to who was the fastest bowler has intrigued and entertained enthusiasts at all levels of the game. England, following on the magnificance of Tom Richardson, have had Kortright, Larwood, 'Typhoon' Tyson and 'Fiery' Fred Trueman among the candidates for the distinction.

Australians claim Albert 'Tibby' Cotter – 'the human catapult' he was called – and in more recent years Gregory, McDonald, Lindwall and Miller. There were times in 1928 when Learie Constantine and Martindale of West Indies bowled very fast indeed but, in the 1960s, Wesley Hall at times bowled, perhaps, a couple of yards faster than either of them. South Africa's Heine, Adcock, and Pollock, have produced deliveries which caused the batsman to say on arrival at the dressing-room, 'That was as fast as anything I've ever seen', or even to admit, 'I never saw it'.

In that last expression, 'I never saw it', there is, for the cricketer, the real answer to the whole question of speed. What does it matter whether a bowler delivers at 90 m.p.h. (and fast bowling speeds are around this mark) or at 91 m.p.h. if one bowler is performing in the late evening with a darkened pavilion as a background and the other is bowling at midday with a tropical sun directly overhead? How can you compare speeds if one bowler is performing on a pitch like a shirt front, a sandy or wet surface, and the other has a pitch concrete hard, perhaps topped with a stubble of juicy green grass, or on which there has been a slight shower of rain to 'grease' the surface? It is not the m.p.h. that concerns the batsman but the impression of 'hurry' forced upon him in his stroke play that really matters.

Only recently I asked Yorkshire coach Arthur Mitchell, who has seen every bowler since 1921 and played against every one of the so-called fast bowlers in the period between the wars, 'Who was the fastest bowler you ever saw?'

Arthur grinned. He was not to be caught out so easily. 'Don't ask me that,' he said. 'You studied it, but I'll tell you the two occasions when I 'hurried' most.

'The first was at Sheffield in 1928 – I think it was. We won the toss against Nottinghamshire and Harold Larwood bowled us out for 130 runs. I think his figures were 6 wickets for 24 runs in 11 overs and he did it all himself. He didn't want any help. He clean bowled four of us, made a caught and bowled off Percy Holmes, and got an l.b.w. decision. He didn't do it with short pitchers. He kept the ball well up.

'It was the best controlled and fastest bowling I'd ever seen and the only other bowler to make anything of a similar impression was the six-foot-five Ken Farnes at Scarborough in 1932. It was a beautiful pitch. Essex batted first and scored about 330

HAROLD LARWOOD 'He had longish arms, the left shoulder pointed in the direction the ball was intended to go and the shoulder got to the fullest height possible before it started to swing downwards and outwards . . .'

CLARENCE VICTOR GRIMMETT 'Few slow bowlers have had a greater command of length and direction, related to so many different paces, whether back or front of the hand, or right or left arm'

runs by half past five. They declared and got us in for the last half hour. We lost three wickets and might have lost the lot against the bowling of Maurice Nicholls and Farnes.'

Arthur grinned at the recollection. 'Talk about playing at the ball when it was in the wicket-keeper's gloves... it was almost frightening... and yet the very next day the same two bowlers, on the same pitch, were carted all over the place in a scoring spree which brought Sutcliffe and Leyland 102 runs in 7 overs and saw 149 scored in 55 minutes.

'Farnes was hit further and more often than Nicholls, he was hit for 75 runs in 4 overs, and yet the previous evening he had made this impression on me. I suppose Larwood in the years I played hurried me most frequently and Farnes certainly did on that occasion.'

This experience by Arthur Mitchell tends to prove my contention that 'hurry' by the batsman is much more important than m.p.h. With the dark background of the houses in Trafalgar Square, at a time when the light was fading, Farnes at Scarborough was tremendous. I will never believe he lost so much pace overnight he was no longer fast. It was just a case that the batsmen next day saw the ball much better – they were not hurried so much.

There are two other reasons for this obvious 'hurry' on the part of the batsmen and the illusion of speed on the part of the bowler.

First, the more steeply the ball leaves the bowler's hand to the place where it bounces on the pitch, the more difficult it is for the batsman to see it. The ball is coming downwards through the line of vision.

As any photographer knows it is possible to take a photograph of an express train coming towards you with an exposure of 1.25th second – and the image will be clear.

But try taking the photograph from a position sideways on with the same exposure – the train going through the line of vision – and see what happens. The whole picture will be a blur.

I was by no stretch of imagination a batsman but I recall once at Trent Bridge when Larwood and Voce (there was no fast bowlers' 'union' in those days) gave me a taste of bouncers.

To my amazement, it being a lovely day and Larwood's hand being little above the level of my eyes when he let go of the ball I found I could see it all the way. At the other end, Voce, much taller and 'digging 'em in', came across the line of vision and the ball seemed to be almost hitting the pitch before I saw it. He pinged me on the hip and ribs time and again, especially because he was a left-hander, bowling round the wicket, and bringing the ball 'in' to me.

It must be remembered that a cricket pitch is only 22 yards long. The batsman stands up the pitch a yard or more towards the bowler. The bowler delivers from his front foot, a yard or more towards the batsman – and at 90 m.p.h. the ball has less than 20 yards to come. Eye specialists say the ball is six or seven yards on its way before the light rays have entered the eye, flashed to the brain and the brain has directed the muscles the action to take. The ball now has only 12 yards to come and the batsman only about one-third of a second for his shot. It is now that the 'hurry' on the part of the batsmen can be appreciated

One also hears it said about a bowler, 'He comes very fast off the pitch'. With a full body-swing it is obvious that a bowler will bring the ball off the pitch quicker than the bowler with a stilted action. But, unless top spin is imparted it is impossible to make a ball leave any surface faster than it goes on. Fast bowlers obviously cannot impart top spin at the moment of release. For them there must be some sort of braking action when the ball pitches.

Speed off the pitch is an optical illusion which occurs when the ball leaves the pitch at a much flatter angle than expected. If you want to prove this, take a ball into the garden and get someone to throw a few half-volleys towards you for fielding practice. You are sure to get cracked on the shins with one that doesn't bounce as much as expected – and you'll get the impression that the ball left the surface faster than it reached it.

If you had a bat in your hand you would have to jab down pretty smartly to stop the ball, and in reverse, if the ball 'popped' unexpectedly (even though this means the ball has dug deeper into the pitch and therefore braked more) you would have to lift the bat very sharply, or think very quickly to get out of the way of the ball. You would be hurried and, again, it is this hurry which is far more important than m.p.h.

As a Yorkshire player it is perhaps natural that I should accept the opinions of tried and proven Yorkshire colleagues in the highest sphere of cricket and in which they made big reputations.

Wilfred Rhodes, who began his career in 1898 and played for 33 seasons, scoring nearly 40,000 runs and taking more than 4,000 wickets, said Larwood bowled faster than any man he ever saw.

In 1937 Herbert Sutcliffe, England's most successful batsman in Tests against Australia, said Larwood was the best fast bowler in England, and in 1944 another of England's great all-rounders, Sir Stanley Jackson, who started his cricket even before Wilfred Rhodes, had this to say: 'Although I never played against him, Larwood appeared to me the best fast bowler I ever saw.

'I have a great admiration for him with his beautiful rhythmic run and perfect action which gave him complete control over pace, direction and length. The Australian Ernest Jones was the best of my time,' said Sir Stanley.

In 1954 'Typhoon' Tyson, under the captaincy of Sir Leonard Hutton, was greatly instrumental in keeping the 'Ashes' for England.

He bowled magnificently. He hurried the batsmen to such an extent he many times hit the blade of the bat before the batsman had started a movement towards the ball. If one could draw a comparison between the bowling of Larwood and Tyson in such infinitesimal fractions of time it would be only to say that Larwood many times hit the bat, or had flashed past, while the batsman was still lifting the bat from the block hole. Australians said Tyson was 'the next fastest thing to Larwood'.

It is rather surprising to think that both these fast bowlers should decide that Australia was the country to adopt when cricket days ended. Larwood moved out with wife and family in 1950, and now says he would have gone years earlier if he had had any sense. The ill-feeling of the 'Bodyline Tour' has gone. Larwood is remembered and accepted as a great bowler of former days and as a man – a quiet, retiring man, shrinking from any type of publicity, delighted when any of his former friends call to see him, but not prepared to cross the road to see them – in case he was not welcome. Few people would reconcile the Larwood of today with the fast bowling terror of 1932–33. But for that matter few people who knew Larwood as a boy, not even his own father, conceived the ability that was his. His fame was upon them almost before they had realised.

Harold Larwood was born at Nuncargate, a mining village in

Nottinghamshire on November 19th, 1904. Unlike his brothers Philip, Robert and Ernest who were all music-minded, Harold had only one passion. He wanted to play cricket. His father, a former captain of the village team, was responsible for this. He carved him a bat from a piece of wood when the boy was only two years old. He cut him larger bats as the boy grew up but growing up was something that seemed to dodge young Larwood. When he was thirteen and went to work in the local grocer's shop, weighing out flour, he was only four feet high and little bigger than the sacks he tried to pull around. He was found unconscious one day under a hundredweight pack of margarine he had been trying to move.

At fourteen he went down the pit as a pony driver and father, trying to get him interested in something other than cricket, and to earn a shilling or two extra, sent him to the local golf club to act as a caddie.

It did not have the desired effect. Neither did night shift work at Langton Colliery when, after three years as a pit boy, he left Annesley to work at the coal face. Stripped to the waist, with a clearance of no more than three feet, he had to clean the face – lay bare the coal seam for the daytime workers. The boy surfaced with only one thought in mind, to play cricket.

At 15 he played in the Nuncargate 2nd XI as a fast bowler. He was with the first team at 17, bowling in sand shoes because he could not afford cricket boots, and it was in cricket he found the mental relaxation and change from the hard picking at the coal face.

Living a few doors away from the Larwoods was the former Nottinghamshire and England player, Joe Hardstaff whose son 'Young Joe' followed him. He noted the keenness of the young Larwood and, hearing rumours that Nottinghamshire were considering enlarging their staff and joining the 2nd XI championship, told the officials he knew a young fast bowler who might interest them.

'Bring him along,' he was told, 'We'll give him a trial at the nets.'

Joe saw Harold's father and persuaded him to spend £9 to fit the boy out with boots and clothes, and on a never-to-be-forgotten day in early 1923, when the lad was eighteen, he and his father accompanied Joe to Trent Bridge – the boy's third visit to the ground. In previous years he had seen Notts play Warwickshire and Surrey.

He was only five-feet-four at this time, slightly built and pasty faced as a result of his work in the mines. He was watched with some interest and not a little amusement as he measured out his twenty-pace run-up but, like the famous advertisement for piano lessons, they looked in amazement when he began to play. Harold said to me one day, recalling the occasion, 'I must have looked a real greenhorn in my new clobber'.

Anyhow he got signed on a season's trial at thirty-two shillings a week, the same as he got for a week's work down the pit, and Jim Iremonger, the county coach took him under his wing. He had to help in the pavilion, clean the dressing-rooms and clean the boots. Maurice Tate once tipped him a couple of bob for doing this job during one of his visits to Trent Bridge. Little did either think they would be opening the bowling together for England in a few years time.

The Trent Bridge pitch has always been known as a featherbed surface, ideal for run-making and a heartbreak for the bowlers. So much so that, when after the second world war there was a general outcry for faster and more sporting surfaces, the groundstaff were unable to supply requirements, and eventually it was decided to remove all of the top soil from the playing square.

Young Larwood, to try and overcome the ease of the pitches, had to strive for yet more and more pace and weld to it the other essentials of good bowling. With a good eye and a deceptive wiry strength he showed signs of being a good type of forcing batsman, too.

He found encouragement in August 1924 when Nottinghamshire selected him to play his first big game against Northamptonshire. He did not do very well. He bowled 26 overs to take 1 wicket for 71 runs. His first victim was Vallance Jupp whom he bowled after scoring 23 runs. In the second XI averages he had 35 wickets at 13.14 each.

The turning point in Larwood's career came in June 1925 when he played for the Nottinghamshire second XI against Lancashire 2nd at Kirkby. Notts, skittled out for 155 and 46, were beaten by 10 wickets but, in the Lancashire first innings of 198 runs, Larwood had 8 wickets for 44. It was a performance which took him straight into the senior side – and he never looked back.

At the end of the season he had taken 73 wickets in first-class cricket at a cost of 18 runs each and had one outstanding match against Worcestershire when he claimed 11 wickets for 41. He got his county cap, and two matches later he made 70 in a partnership with Wilf Payton which put on 151 runs in 110 minutes for the eighth wicket against Northants. Larwood's chief memory of that season, however, is that after being picked for the first team he played against Yorkshire and his first victim was Herbert Sutcliffe who was caught in the slips by the Notts captain, A. W. Carr. In the report on the season *Wisden* in its usual factual style said, 'Larwood made good his claims to a regular place in the Nottinghamshire side'. As a batsman he played 27 innings, was not out 12 times, and averaged 24.

Now firmly established in the Nottinghamshire side and producing performances to keep him there, Larwood's next honour came in early June 1926 when he was chosen to play for the North of England against the Australians at Birmingham. He captured three wickets in the match, Mailey in the first innings, Woodfull and Taylor in the second. This was followed by his selection for the second Test at Lord's when he shared the new ball with Maurice Tate and the specialist leg-theory or in-swing-bowler, Fred Root.

He did not produce anything out of the ordinary. The Lord's pitch was like every other surface in the country, lifeless, made for batting, and in a drawn game Larwood had 2 wickets for 99 and 1 for 37. The Australian Warren Bardsley, making his fourth trip to England, scored 173 not out.

Larwood's first Test wicket was Macartney, caught by Herbert Sutcliffe in the slips, and later in the innings he bowled Gregory. The major satisfaction for the England bowlers came from the fact that they were not alone in their toil. The Australian bowlers experienced it, too, with Hobbs scoring 119 and Patsy Hendren 127 not out.

A hat-trick against Cambridge University just before the team for the third Test at Leeds was announced did not tip the scales in Larwood's favour. He did not appear for England again until the last game of the series at the Oval where, after four drawn matches, everything was set for a decider. This was the game in which Wilfred Rhodes at the age of 48 was recalled to the England side and Percy Chapman took over the England captaincy.

In the first innings England scored 280 and Australia 302. Larwood, sharing the new ball with Tate, had 3 for 82 and Tate 3 for 40. Rain came and England, facing a deficit of 22 runs and a 'sticky' wicket, were in serious trouble. But Hobbs and Sutcliffe produced one of their finest partnerships. Hobbs made 100, Sutcliffe 161, and England totalled 436. More rain fell just before the end of the England innings and this was followed by hot sunshine. It was Australia who were now in trouble, how much trouble can be judged from the fact that they started batting at half past three on the fourth day and the match was all over at six. Larwood 3 for 34, Rhodes 4 for 44, Tate, Geary and Stevens one apiece, routed the Australians for 125 runs. England had won the Ashes and Larwood, with 6 wickets for 116 runs in the match, received high commendation.

His season's work brought him 137 wickets at 18.3 each and at the end of this, his first full season, *Wisden* named him as one of its 'Five Cricketers of the Year'. Larwood had made his mark. He finished top of the Notts bowling averages with 96 wickets.

Although the year 1927 did not see any great leap forward in the performances of the twenty-two-year-old Larwood, it saw steady consolidation and was an important year in his life. This was the year that a tall – over six-foot slow left-arm bowler Bill Voce joined the Nottinghamshire groundstaff. He was a pale faced, gangling youth. There was not much timber on him. Yet, he had a powerful frame and it did not take officials at Trent Bridge long to realise that, if they could build him up, get plenty of red meat into him, they had an ideal fast-bowling partner for Larwood. It was not long before the partnership of Larwood and Voce, opening the attack for Nottinghamshire and England, became as famous as any in the history of the game, Gregory and McDonald, Lindwall and Miller, and, in later years, Statham and Trueman.

Larwood at this time had been nursed along by his county captain Arthur Carr with skill and consideration. He was rarely called upon to bowl more than four or five overs in a spell. Carr was at pains not to overtax the strength or stamina of his young bowler. But, towards the end of the season, playing in a game for The Rest against England, the captain of The Rest XI gave Larwood a dozen overs on the trot. Lol was convinced that the unaccustomed strain set up cartilage trouble.

At the end of the season Larwood was quietly married to Lois Bird, a young woman from the neighbouring village of Huthwaite, and his usual dislike for fuss and publicity ensured that the wedding was a registry office affair, with everybody sworn to secrecy and only the nearest members of the families present.

The cartilage trouble did not clear up with treatment. The doctors advised an operation to have it out. The Nottinghamshire club agreed and Lol came home from nursing home to join his young wife on Christmas Eve. He had about four months to strengthen his left leg again for the job of fast bowling, take the full jar of the delivery action, and the full strain of the pivot and swing away to the off-side of the pitch, following the delivery stride.

How well he did it is best explained by saying he finished top of the England bowling averages with 138 wickets at 14 apiece. He played for England against the touring West Indies side and, in the Test at Lord's, the first time I had met him, he put on a show I am not likely to forget.

I remember looking at this slightly built, almost schoolboyish youngster, with the mop of hair which seemed to stand straight up and without a parting, almost in disbelief. Surely this could not be the fast bowling terror? Only after the initial surprise did one notice the strong neck, powerful shoulders, and the lithe grace with which he moved round the dressing-room. Following on some fine fast-bowling by Learie Constantine, who also gave the best exhibition of fielding I have ever seen in my life, I recall Larwood generating such speed that he flicked the peak of F. R. Martin's cap and turned it round almost before the batsman had decided on a shot. Another delivery struck the same batsman on the forehead, fortunately without doing any real damage, and then George Challenor got down to Larwood's end and had his cap turned from back to front with yet another delivery which lifted at tremendous speed. I was a youngster on the M.C.C. groundstaff at the time and hoping one day I might be a fast bowler. Never before had I seen anything like Connie or Lol in that game, and some years later when I was chatting with Larwood I mentioned this match to him. Without any sort of emotion in his voice, as if merely stating a fact, he said, 'Oh, yes. I remember. I was nursing my knee after a cartilage operation for most of that summer, but umpire Frank Chester said something to me about fast bowling and I decided to let one or two go.'

He was chosen to go to Australia with Percy Chapman's 1928-29 tour – the only fast bowler in the team – and Lol told me that on the hard grounds of Australia he found it necessary to 'nurse' his leg along. I don't doubt he did find it necessary in some small degree, but his performances hardly suggested he was hanging back. In the third important game of the tour, against Victoria, he took 7 wickets for 51 runs in one innings.

He was chosen to play in the first Test, to be played on the new Woolloongabba ground at Brisbane and he scored 70 runs and shared a record 8th wicket stand putting on 124 runs with Patsy Hendren. He followed this by claiming 6 wickets for 32 runs to see Australia skittled out for 122 runs in reply to England's first innings total of 521. He scored another 37 runs in the second innings, claimed another 2 wickets for 30 runs, and also made four catches. England's victory by 675 runs was one of the biggest on record and Larwood's contribution to the victory quite outstanding. Don Bradman played his first Test against England in this game but after scoring 18 and 1, he was not chosen for the next game.

England won the second Test, at Sydney by eight wickets, retained the Ashes with a victory at Melbourne when Hobbs and Sutcliffe gave yet another brilliant exhibition of 'sticky wicket' batsmanship, and then went on to a twelve-run victory in the fourth Test. Critics noted that Larwood cut his run down by six yards in the fifth Test which Australia won by five wickets – a game in which Bradman scored 123 and Woodfull 102. This was perhaps the real extent to which Larwood rested his knee apart from the minor matches of the tour. He proved himself a truly great fast bowler and very nearly a fine all-rounder. He made useful runs, and was an agile fieldsman with a safe pair of hands.

It is difficult to convey to present day cricketers the batting perfection of pitches in England in the period between the wars. Runs were the true measure of the groundsman's art. The pitch at Trent Bridge where Larwood did most of his bowling was known as the best batting surface in the world. 'Bosser' Martin at the Oval had a surface known as the graveyard of the slow left-hander. Jack White at Lord's and 'Dicky' Moulton at Leeds, knew every trick of the trade. They knew exactly how much marl to use to bind the surface to prevent crumbling, the right quantity of yellow clay to stop the rain percolating, and how much cow manure was needed to take out the 'life'.

These groundsmen were not content to take off the grass with a finely set hand cutter. Fast bowlers got help from green grass. They got on their hands and knees and shaved it off. Rarely did a pitch show green before a Test match. They were bare, lifeless strips, without pace and bounce, and where even the speed of Larwood failed to make the best batsmen really 'hurry'. To try and induce errors the fast bowlers of the time, especially the big ones like Bill Voce, Ken Farnes and myself, had to rely largely on the 'bouncer'. This was a useful delivery if you could bowl one unexpectedly or if you could make a good batsman expect one and you delivered a half-volley instead. It had intimidatory value against inferior batsmen, but on English Test pitches, I fancy that any of the first five batsmen in an international side would gladly have paid half-a-crown a time for bouncers.

Larwood's bowling had such excellence he was always round about the top of the bowling averages, and indeed, he took the first position in five out of ten seasons from 1927. But like almost every other type of bowler, when bowling to the best players in the world on English pitches, he had to hope that the groundsman had made an error, left a little bit too much dampness in the pitch, or had been prevented by the weather from putting the finishing touches to his creation.

The South Africans who toured England in 1929 found they could deal with Larwood quite comfortably, but it took the visit of the Australians in 1930, and in particular the brilliance of the young Don Bradman, to demonstrate how friendly and easy-paced the pitches really were. Bradman dominated a series which Australia won by two games to one, two matches drawn. In the first Test he scored 131; in the second 254; in the third at Leeds with 100 before lunch, 100 before tea, and another 100 before close of play, he made 334; and after failure in the fourth he finished with an innings of 232 in the fifth, at the Oval.

Bradman in the Test matches scored 974 runs at an average of 139 an innings. Woodfull, Ponsford, Kippax, Fairfax, all averaged over 50, and Larwood who played in two Tests and bowled 101 overs had 4 wickets at 73 apiece to show for his efforts. Larwood went back to his county side and seemed to be forgotten. Against the New Zealanders in 1931 and India in 1932 (who were given their first Test at Lord's) the selectors, seeking to encourage other fast bowlers, tried G. O. Allen, Bill Voce and myself. The four of us were chosen to make the tour to Australia under the captaincy of D. R. Jardine in the winter of 1932–33.

In the meantime I had met, and been accepted by, the Notts captain Arthur Carr. I was introduced to him by the former Yorkshire bowler George Macaulay, and I shall always remember the way he ignored my outstretched hand, eyed me up and down, and said with a sneer in his voice, 'And you think you're a fast bowler. I've got the only two in England, Larwood and Voce.' He then turned his back on me.

To play at Trent Bridge against Notts in those days was an education. When Yorkshire were the visitors any spectator arriving after 11 a.m. was without a seat or had to separate from his friends to take what was going. One could feel the expectancy in the air. If a batsman played at a Larwood or Voce delivery without touching it, at least 10,000 spectators would appeal for a catch behind. If a Larwood express sent a stump cartwheeling the roar could be heard for miles.

On the day of this meeting with Carr, Yorkshire fielded, and I managed to take a few wickets. Arthur Carr came to the dressing-room, walked across to me, and holding out his hand, said: 'There's three. Every Monday night I take Bill and Lol out for a meal and a drink. I want you to join us. Say you will.'

I did. I went out with them once or twice and Arthur Carr fed us on great big steaks and as much beer as we could take.

Lol told me one day. 'Skipper thinks the world of Bill and me. He thinks all fast bowlers should train on beer... and he thinks you want proper feeding for the job. He takes us out twice a week and he always pays.' At this stage Lol turned to his pal Voce for moral support and said, 'Doesn't he, Bill?' Bill picked up his pint, took a good long drink, and then said, 'Aye. And when we're thirsty it costs him a bob or two.'

When D. R. Jardine was made captain for the tour to Australia he spent a great deal of time with Arthur Carr, particularly trying to find out how Arthur got that little bit of something extra out of his two bowlers. He was no doubt told, 'You can lead 'em anywhere but you can't drive 'em an inch. Lol is better used in short spells. Bill can do a long one if you want it.'

D. R. J. did not subscribe to the Carr beer treatment. At close of play in all the important matches he used to detail two of the players to stick with Harold for the rest of the evening and it was their duty to see it was an abstemious evening and early to bed. I usually did duty with Maurice Leyland in this regard. We soon found out that we couldn't drive Larwood and, when it came to leading him Bill Voce had us skinned. Many and many a time he came to the assistance of the detailed players.

The big scoring by the Australian batsmen, and in particular Don Bradman, during the 1930 tour of England was something that Jardine intended to counter if it was at all possible. He was certain the Australians had such an all-round ability to make strokes that it was impossible to bowl to them using a standardised 4/5 field placing. That is, five men on the off, four on the leg, or vice versa. He wanted a 7/2 field placing if possible and nothing more than a 6/3. 'You must bowl a definite leg-theory or off-theory. You must attack off stump and just outside, or you must attack leg stump and just outside,' he said. 'By confining stroke play to one half of the field we can contain the batsmen. My chief concern is whether you bowlers can produce the control needed,' he added.

Jardine, a man who planned his every move like a chess player, had no intention of revealing his tactics too early. In the opening match of the tour against Western Australia he only gave Larwood six overs of off-theory and in the second game of the tour against a Combined XI when four of Australia's batting stars (including Bradman) were in the opposition he faced them with all the slow bowlers and G. O. Allen. But he only gave Allen four overs in the first innings and seven in the second.

In the third game of the tour, against South Australia, he only gave Larwood five overs and did not play him against Victoria; but then brought him in for the fifth game, against a Combined XI in which both Woodfull and Bradman figured for the opposition. Jardine had Larwood start with off-theory and against Bradman he switched to leg theory. He had Voce and myself try both theories, too, but it was Larwood who took the eye. I say this purely and simply as a bowler judging another – Larwood was magnificent. He had a spot-on accuracy in direction. He could switch easily from off-stump to leg stump attack... and at what a terrific pace!

Larwood seemed to skim off the hard Bulli soil surfaces of Australia like a pebble skimming off water and with a bounce equally unpredictable. He had such pace that any delivery pitching more than half-way down the pitch was good length. He had the additional great asset (which he said he noticed on his first trip to Australia) that whereas most deliveries would go flashing through at less than stump height, one out of every three or four deliveries would skim off the surface to be chest height at the batsman. He did not have to dig the ball in deliberately. It happened naturally. If Voce, Allen or myself wanted to make the ball get chest height at the batsman we had to dig it in, and it bounced like a tennis ball and with all the speed taken out of it.

Lol skimmed 'em, and to such purpose he claimed four wickets for 54 runs in the first innings and two wickets for five runs in four overs in the second. He got Bradman out in both innings and the Don confessed later he disliked the method of Larwood's attack so much he immediately complained to the Australian selectors present at the match.

Jardine, and the England players, were delighted. The skipper had really hit upon something good and the first Test match, even though Stan McCabe hit leg theory all over the Sydney Oval for a not out score of 187, did nothing to quell that delight. All the other batsmen failed. England went to a ten-wicket win and Larwood in the two innings had 5 for 96 and 5 for 28... wonderful bowling.

Flushed with success, Jardine decided to play all of his four fast bowlers in the second Test, but the Melbourne groundsman proved too wily. On a pitch that crumbled badly, a century by Bradman and some fine slow bowling by Bill O'Reilly saw Australia through to a win by 111 runs. Yet, England's bowling on this unsuitable pitch had seen Australia out for 228 and 191. There was still a lot to be said for the theory of attack.

A lot to be said! A hard pitch at Adelaide for the third Test, with Larwood again finding that disconcerting 'skim' saw the start of a controversy which split cricketers and administrators the world over. One delivery from Larwood pinged Woodfull over the heart and sent the Australian skipper reeling. Bertie Oldfield, going for a pull stroke at Larwood, deflected the ball to his right temple and it felled him like an ox. Prior to this Fingleton and Ponsford had taken knock after knock high on the thighs – and in the middle of the back, too, as they had tried to get away from the 'skimmers'. The crowd went mad. They hooted and booed. An Australian journalist coined the word 'Bodyline'. Amid scenes never before seen on a cricket ground England won by 338 runs (Larwood seven wickets in the match) and cables between the Australian Board of Control and M.C.C. brought an offer from M.C.C. to cancel the tour immediately.

Jardine called a meeting of his players and asked if they wanted him to abandon his ideas of off-theory and leg-theory bowling. They voted overwhelmingly to have it continued. With Larwood as the spearhead of the attack, claiming 33 wickets at 19.5 each on the tour, England took the series by four-one. Wherever Larwood played there were packed grounds. Larwood's 'skim' was unpleasant for batsmen but my word it was thrilling to watch.

On the tour Larwood got Bradman out six times in ten meetings. The Don's average, from 139 an innings during the tour of England was reduced to 56.5 an innings on this tour by England. Of course, other batsmen and bowlers, especially Allen, had moments of glory. Jardine, for his unswerving approach to the job of beating Australia, deserved special praise. But the real hero of the piece was Larwood. He rounded off the series by scoring 98 in the first innings of the fifth Test and how those Australian barrackers 'rose' to him. Although they booed and jeered and shouted, they knew his worth. They loved him. He had great entertainment value.

Unfortunately, the jar on the hard grounds damaged the great toe joint on Larwood's left foot. He was sent home for treatment instead of going on to New Zealand with the rest of the M.C.C. team. Although the furore of Bodyline was still raging in official circles, Nottinghamshire supporters showed what they thought of Larwood when he arrived at Nottingham station at midnight April 9, 1933. There were 20,000 cheering fans to meet him.

Alas, rest and treatment did not bring a cure for Larwood. He only bowled ten overs for Notts that season and, in October, he went to hospital for an operation on the injured foot. M.C.C. paid the cost of the operation £163 and the insurance company paid £222. Unfortunately the operation was only partly successful. Larwood returned to first-class cricket in 1934 but he was no longer the greatest fast bowler. He put on a show of leg-theory for the spectators at Maurice Leyland's benefit match at Leeds in 1934, just for a couple of overs – and I recall now how the huge crowd cheered and cheered again at the thrill of it. But it was the Australians who had seen Larwood at his best. As a fast medium bowler he took 82 wickets in 1934, 102 in 1935, and in 1936, when he got £2,000 from his benefit match with Yorkshire, he again topped the England bowling averages with 119 wickets at 12 apiece!

He took a coaching job in India for the winter but he didn't like the treatment he got and he decided to come back after three weeks! In August 1937 the Nottinghamshire club suspended him for failing to attend the ground for practice... he was still hard to drive!

Lol finished with the first-class game in 1938 and concentrated on growing flowers and vegetables in Nottingham as a week-day job and playing for Blackpool at cricket on Saturday afternoons. In his career he had taken 1,427 wickets at 17.5 apiece.

In 1945, when the war ended, he bought a sweet and tobacco shop in Blackpool and then, five years later, staggered all his friends by announcing that he was off to Australia with his wife Lois and his five daughters. It was equally surprising to know that Jack Fingleton, one of the batsmen Larwood knocked about with leg-theory, was the man who delightedly made it possible. To Larwood's surprise (when he found out) it was Australian Labour Prime Minister Mr Ben Chifley, a keen cricketer, who out of his own pocket paid half of Larwood's weekly hotel bill until his house at Randwick, Sydney, was ready for occupation. No wonder Lol thought that Fingleton had fixed him with a very good and very cheap hotel!

Larwood had many jobs offered him. Australian businessmen were prepared to pay for his name, but Larwood would have none of that. 'I'd rather shovel muck than have a charity job,' he told me. It was perhaps as well he did not know of Mr Chifley's kindness.

He got a job as a night watchman and then as a storekeeper. Few people now know him as the greatest fast bowler of all time, centre of the game's greatest controversy, and whose great accuracy brought legislation against intimidatory bowling. Larwood likes to be unknown and he has found great happiness.

In the 35 years since 'bodyline' I have seen every fast bowler of reputation in the world. I have not seen one with the speed or the perfection of action of Larwood. I have never seen another bowler 'skim' from Australian pitches like Larwood. He could not get it in England and I often wonder if the legislators did not rule against all fast bowlers because of a merit possessed by one bowler only. To have seen Larwood in Australia is to have witnessed one of the greatest of all sporting occasions.

FOUR

Grimmett and O'Reilly
by Ian Peebles

1

THE GOOGLY may be regarded as just another of those British inventions, neglected at home, but recognised and developed abroad. It was, as we all know, invented by Bosanquet as a result of messing about on a billiard table. A number of people had, intentionally or inadvertently, made the leg-break slip through straight, or come a wee bit the other way, amongst them W. G. and A. G. Steel. No one had yet been able to make the ball break from the off with, ostensibly, a leg-break action, *at will*, until Bosanquet suddenly loosed what was tantamount to chemical warfare on the well-schooled, unsuspecting batsmen of the day. But this success sprang from novelty rather than efficiency.

The googly made little progress in England. The inventor, after limited success, finished his days as a fast-medium seamer and found only one true disciple at the moment of truth. This was Reggie Schwartz who was a somewhat unsatisfactory prophet in two senses. In the first place he found that, having mastered the secret of the 'bosie', he could not produce its complementary leg-break and that, the more he tried, the more the darn thing turned from the off. This caused him much irritation and disposed of all element of deception and, one might have thought, of effectiveness. But Aubrey Faulkner used to say that, so unnatural did this off-breaking leg-break appear to the uninitiated, they just could not bring themselves to believe it would or could happen. Also, Schwartz was intrinsically such a good off-break bowler, with a steep dropping flight, and a nip and turn that was beyond the scope of the orthodox front of the hand cut. The other snag to Schwartz as a disciple was that, having acquired the art, he started a species of 'googly brain drain' by departing for South Africa. Few Englishmen seriously pursued the perfecting of the googly and, until the first war, only D. W. Carr developed it to workable international standards in England.

In South Africa, the seed Schwartz brought with him took root in startling fashion. Within a few years he was a member of the greatest quartette of wrist spinners yet seen. Vogler, Faulkner, White and Schwartz shook English batsmanship as fundamentally as John Welles had done in the early years of the previous century. The novelty of the 'wrong 'un' still put it at a premium, but it should not be assumed that this was its only virtue in the hands of the South Africans. I saw Faulkner on many occasions, and Vogler on a couple, when both were well past their youth. The quality was still instantly recognisable. They were superb spin bowlers, and one could well see concrete evidence to support Faulkner's opinion that Vogler, at his best, was second only to Barnes amongst the right-handed spinners.

The foursome was sadly short-lived as such and, when it withered, the seed blew not back to the Motherland, but over the Indian Ocean to Australia. There it found its truest and healthiest environment, and there it has excelled all other cultures ever since.

By the 'nineties the wickets to be found in the great Australian centres had fully developed to their intended character. They were hard as steel, and the surface shone as though polished. Cracks might form a fine network, but they had no effect on the swift true progress of the ball. Bowlers had to be accurate, enduring and hopeful. The only disturbing factors they could introduce, in good weather, were abnormal pace or prodigious spin. The latter might not immediately cause the ball to deviate but it might induce it to do things in the air, and it could cause it to bounce. The googly added a further dimension to these possibilities, and it was eagerly seized upon. From this point there ran an almost uninterrupted succession of Australian 'bosie' bowlers, better than any contemporary rival power could produce at any given moment. And at this particular moment there are signs that the line, rather tenuously sustained by Bobby Simpson, is about to be renewed by a bunch of virile young leg tweakers just coming up.

In addition to those who made fame playing for Australia there was a great number playing in all grades of cricket and some, like Matthews, Emery, and Trenerry, who flitted about on the fringe of greatness. The individuals who composed the main stream were interesting men, as well as fascinating craftsmen.

The first of the line was Horden, for Armstrong was not, strictly speaking, of the genus. Horden was a dentist by profession who studied in Philadelphia and served an apprenticeship with that distinguished club. He was a magnificent bowler, of length, adequate pace, and an abundance of well disguised spin. In an Australian side which lost 4–1 in 1911–12 he took 32 wickets for 24 apiece. Plum Warner thought him the best of the 'bosies' but whether when he came to this conclusion, he had seen O'Reilly is not clear. Again he might, arguably, not regard O'Reilly as a googly bowler in the accepted sense of the term.

Mailey, whose death is so widely lamented as I write, was a splendid link in the chain, of wit, and whimsy, and truly prodigious spin. He originally made a very good duet with Armstrong, whose unflagging accuracy and restrained degree of spin made a perfect foil to Mailey's occasionally erratic fireworks. Later Mailey and Grimmett shared the 'bosie' department, but this was a short-lived association. The greatest leg spin and googly combination was yet to come.

2

Clarence Victor Grimmett was born in Dunedin on Christmas Day; a statement which smacks of Dickens or the Brothers Grimm. This was in 1892 and in a few years' time the lad was playing for Mount Cook Boys School in Wellington as a fast bowler. Any mind which ever pitted itself against Clarrie in later years can but boggle at this thought, and would probably have preferred him to have stayed that way. Apparently it was a certain Mr Hempelman (again the faintly outlandish flavour) who taught and inspired him to bowl slow leg-breaks. *Wisden* records that in the early stages of their association Clarrie disregarded Mr H.'s express directions and bowled fast against Wairarapa to take 7 wickets for 3 runs. The writer makes no actual comment, but it is clear from a certain primness in his words that he is at a loss to explain how such mutinous conduct could meet with such tremendous and unmerited reward. 'Still', he continues, 'Mr Hempelman persevered with him' and now the moral is clearly drawn.

Despite Mr Hempelman's perseverance, many more of Clarrie's years were to be expended in trying to convince the world of cricket that he was a serious bowler. Although he got results he never really looked the part. Thus grudgingly recognised in his native New Zealand, he moved to Sydney. There he got as far as grade cricket but then, prospects of State cricket seeming remote, he moved on to Melbourne. Here he did better and was picked for Victoria against New South Wales at Sydney, but failed to get a single wicket. After a long wait he played again, this time against South Australia, and got 8 wickets in their second innings. Perhaps the home side spoke encouraging words, or perhaps he took a liking to Adelaide. At any rate he cast in his lot with his late opponents, and stayed with them for the rest of his cricketing days.

Here again he had to persevere in order to gain due recognition. When it came it led to immediate sensation. If the climb had been long and hard, the arrival was triumphant. In 1925 England had won a Test match against Australia for the first time since 1912, and the news from Melbourne field resounded throughout England to arouse hopes that a great period of English cricket had been initiated. This defeat, coupled with the fact that the series was safely won, may have induced a rather conservative Australian Selection Committee to experiment. The persistent and industrious Grimmett was included in the team for the last Test, at Sydney. As all the world knows, he bowled England out twice, given no help on the first occasion, and just a little from rain on the second. He took 11 wickets for 82 runs and England lost by 307 runs. It was as though a nanny had quelled an over-exuberant child with one good resounding smack.

There was naturally great curiosity when this tweaking carnivore arrived in England the following year. He did not look very fierce. In appearance and action he might have popped out of a fairy tale. He was small, bald and bright-eyed, and he hopped, and skipped, and spun industriously with a strange, low, flailing right arm. I went to see him bowl at Lords in 1926 with Aubrey Faulkner. That great judge of the game was much surprised by what he saw and, after an over or two, shook his head and said, 'That won't do at all.' Clarrie, it seems, had a flair for deceiving and dis-impressing good judges as well as bad.

There was certainly good reason for Faulkner's reservations. At first in England Clarrie looked rather a stereotyped round-armer, with a penchant for top spin. The fact remains that he was a jolly good bowler in 1926 but not yet, with the know-how he had acquired on that trip, the superb bowler he was when he returned in 1930. His reputation was then so established that people forgot that he did not look very special.

He was a remarkably accurate bowler. Few slow bowlers have had a greater command of length and direction, related to so many different paces, whether back or front of the hand, or right or left arm. He was not a prodigious spinner like Arthur Mailey, but his leg-break turned sharply where it could bite. His 'bosie' was not a particularly deadly example of its species, but useful for tactical and propaganda purposes. The top spinner was a *very* good ball, delivered a bit quicker and with a tendency to dip in late in flight. These three balls were basically his whole gamut for, possibly mindful of Mr Hempelman, he never bowled a quick one. The permutations he could achieve from these three primary accomplishments, by skilful variations of pace and flight, were infinite. And he had a shrewd eye for which mixture was the most suitable for the target of the moment. To the leaden footed he would give the ball plenty of air, but signs of aggression were countered by the flat, swifter top-spinner. His whole approach was professorial, but none the less determined because of that – surgical might, in fact, be a more precisely descriptive term. If he got cross, he never gave way to the ordinary, mortal bowler's gnashing and wailing. The only recorded show of petulance was an occasion when, in mid-over, Bill Woodfull recommended some alteration to the field. This, Clarrie averred, was responsible for the ensuing full toss (a most unusual lapse) for, as he testily related, the suggestion had 'disturbed his concentration'.

In 1930 Clarrie conducted the spin department pretty well single-handed for the supporting slow-bowling fell well short of expectations. Thus, despite the very high class faster bowling of Wall and Fairfax, the bowling of the side as a whole was something of a one-man band. But, as a distinguished English batsman once said of himself in the moment of crisis, 'Cometh the hour, cometh the man'.

3

William Joseph O'Reilly was also a December child, born on the 20th of that month in 1905. By the 'twenties he had grown to be a tall, lanky youth and, like his future partner, originally had ambitions to be a fast bowler. But he, too, soon realised that some abatement in pace was small sacrifice to make towards the development of a real talent for spinning the ball. O'Reilly's methods were largely self-taught, and acquired by observation and his own kind of imitation. The final result of these imitations was a product so unlike the orthodox leg-break bowler that he could hardly be said to belong to any particular type of bowler. Like Barnes, with whom he is inevitably and frequently compared, he was unique.

Until he was eighteen O'Reilly played cricket up-country in the Goulburn district. Don Bradman, although more than a couple of years younger, was active in the same circles so the two knew each other from early days. Fortune swayed to and fro in their encounters. One Saturday afternoon, the first of a two-Saturday fixture, Don batted the whole half-day to be 200 not out at the close. When he took guard, to resume the slaughter the following week, O'Reilly bowled him clean, first ball of the day. So their careers advanced in parallel, and they later played together for New South Wales Second XI.

Whereas Grimmett had to depend on solid material success to impress the sages that he was a real proposition, everyone who saw or played O'Reilly seems to have agreed that here was a special prospect, maybe a world beater. In his early days he played under the captaincy of Reg Bettington, a great character and a great all round sportsman. In the evening they went out to a club to replace the physical and spiritual expenditure of the day. Reg caused his companions to smile sceptically when he indicated the tall but unknown figure of O'Reilly leaning against a pillar with a glass of beer in his hand. 'There,' he said, 'is the greatest bowler in the world.' It was a very shrewd pleasantry.

In the season of 1931-32 O'Reilly fortunes went forward with a rush. He played in the last five Sheffield Shield matches for his State and, this time, made such an impression that he was picked for the final two Test Matches against the visiting South Africans.

As in the case of many successful partnerships, the actual partners were unalike in a great many respects. Where Grimmett was short and slight, O'Reilly was tall and robust. Where the one was studious of mien and gently unostentatious in action, the other was fiery and impulsive, and rather spectacular. To Clarrie, batsmen were an interesting but not unlikeable species to be gently snared. To O'Reilly they were a hostile and frequently irritating bunch, to be charged and remorselessly borne down. Whereas Clarrie, as related, found that annoyance disturbed his concentration, O'Reilly welcomed the rise of righteous indignation as lending strength to his arm. So the combination worked in harmony and unison, method and decorous efficiency at one end and thunderous, sustained assault at the other. Before yielding to the joy of recalling some of the O'Reilly legends it is necessary to give some idea of the mechanics of this stirring performance for the benefit of those readers who did not have the chance of seeing them at first hand.

As I have indicated, it is hardly accurate to describe O'Reilly as a leg-tweaker or a 'bosie'. He was based on a much wider scale than these descriptions would suggest. Maurice Leyland once recalled that the first over he ever received from O'Reilly contained eight balls, each one different in type from the other. The only quality common to the lot was that they were extremely accurate, and each was delivered with a fine venom.

As with Barnes, the basis of the whole operation was the leg-break, in this case delivered at medium pace. Although the wrist was curled to full extent at the start of the swing, at the moment of delivery it was much straighter than, say, that of Mailey or Wright. The resulting delivery was possibly more 'rolled' than spun, but it had plenty of turn on dusty or soft turf, and the disconcerting quality of occasional turn on the hardest Australian pitches. Batsmen would tell you they could see the ball turning over in its flight, but for the most part coming straight on. Every now and again, however, one would go enough to beat the bat though, generally, not enough to miss the stumps. Walter Robins remembers the last ball before lunch on a perfect Melbourne wicket, pitching about middle and leg. He picked it correctly as the leg spinner and played right forward as he thought on top, and covering it completely. He was dismayed to hear Bert Oldfield say 'Well bowled, Bill', and see his off bail tickled out of its groove.

The top-spinner O'Reilly spun rather more, and his 'wrong 'un' he really buzzed. Every ball he bowled had a springing, bouncing quality which naturally grew more pronounced the greater the purchase afforded by the pitch.

The fact that the wrist was fairly straight at the moment of delivery was of rather personal interest to me for, in a modest way, I had a similar technique. I found that the result was that I was inclined to roll rather than spin the leg-break, spin the top one, and was able to give the googly a real tweak. Pundits, usually with no practical experience of their subject, exhorted me to *spin* the leg-break, saying that otherwise I would never make a bowler. I have always believed that it was in my endeavours to follow this advice that I finally damaged a shoulder beyond repair (at least until surgery had advanced to post-war levels). Once I got talking to Bill about this and he told me that, on arrival at Sydney, he was told by various wiseacres that he would never be a bowler until he *spun* the leg-break. An outspoken man all his days, O'Reilly replied courteously but firmly to his mentors. 'Then I won't be a bloody bowler,' he said.

How wise he turned out to be. The moral here is that, especially allied to the rest of O'Reilly's armament, the rolled leg-break, which turns just enough to beat the bat, and is always accurate enough to hit the castle without conceding encouraging runs, between times, is a better proposition than the spectacular but costly leg-break which bursts like a bomb – but anywhere. This a point to which I shall return when considering the partnership as an entity.

Meantime to continue with O'Reilly's technical properties. His run and action were both inspiring, but neither was in the purely classical mould. When warmed up to the desired point of efficiency, temperamentally and physically, he would stump back his twelve yards purposefully, turn on his mark and, lowering his head, charge. His feet pounded and his arms flailed, but he gathered himself beautifully on the penultimate stride. All, at this moment, was set for a beautiful delivery in the Barnes or Bedser tradition. This Grecian spectacle did not, however, emerge. The bowler turned rather square-on, stooped, and made only negligible use of his left arm. The motion of the right arm, on the other hand, was quite perfect – a long, smooth springlike sling, at full extension throughout. Upon this as much as on any factor, was built the unfailing accuracy of any type of spin or seam the arm was called upon to propel.

The whole performance had a thrashing gusto about it that contributed materially to the final result. Some actions are so smooth and perfect that it is quite easy to follow the progress of the ball from the bowler's first movement at the end of his run. This certainly was a characteristic of Lol Larwood's action and, although I cannot speak from first hand experience, I would suspect that of Lindwall. Any mug could follow the course of the ball clearly until the moment of release. What happened then could, of course, be a different story.

This was not the case with O'Reilly. The flailing arm made the hand hard to follow, and the unusual delivery gave no pre-indication of the pace of the ball about to be discharged. That the speed of the ball bore little relation to the pace of the arm gave an initial advantage, and coupled to the stoop, and the steep drop, accentuated by over spin, it all added up to a peculiar and most puzzling flight. To keep the batsman at the requisite state of tension there was a very good straight quick ball, which shot out at a surprising speed without much warning. The whole operation was spin bowling in its highest expression and, as such, it was a joy to all, not least the recipient if he, too, was a real craftsman.

All this technical excellence was accompanied by a splendid, fiery, unaffected temperament. The approach was good, honest-to-God Irish-Australian, without malice, but red-blooded and certainly without hypocrisy. He huffed and he puffed, and he stamped and he cussed, and his sincerest compliment in recognition of a successful sally on the part of the striker was not 'Jolly good shot, sir', but 'Give me that bloody ball'. No man of understanding or discernment would take offence at this uninhibited evidence of dedication. Many are the tales of O'Reilly's constant battle with what he regarded as a cruelly cynical destiny. Perhaps, a good Irishman at heart, he would prefer 'to take arms against a sea of troubles'.

Personally I have always cherished the recollection of O'Reilly attacking Walter Robins from the Pavilion end at Lords in the Australians *v.* Middlesex match of 1938. The pitch was in the best position the County, as tenants, could claim – right next door to the Test match strip, which is to say between two and three yards to the south of dead centre. Now it was a fact that O'Reilly's googly was very difficult to spot from the hand, but the experienced could pick it, at least sometimes, from the flight as it came out a little higher and slower. On this occasion Walter had not been there very long when he spotted the 'bosie' and, getting down on his right knee he let the bat go. He had guessed right and the ball flew like a homing pigeon into the Tavern. The bowler's indignation was considerable and the next couple of overs were mostly lively paced leg-breaks. But presently along came another 'bosie' and this time the striker wafted it into the tea-room above the bar. This was more than the bowler could be expected to stomach. He called impatiently for the return of the ball and started to walk back to his mark. As he passed the umpire he momentarily found tongue – 'Thought they might play a match like this in the middle!' he snorted.

Jack Fingleton, a contemporary and close friend, provided a rather touching sequel to this tale, illustrative of human nature in the wider sense. It happened at Northampton years afterwards when O'Reilly, now reporting the game, sat in the press box and viewed the match, batsmen included, with a gentle benevolence. So as not to disappoint the vast throng who could not all get in to see the Australians, room was made for some on the grass. But presently this had to be stopped as the square-leg boundary was becoming very short. O'Reilly protested at this prohibition at which Fingleton mildly suggested it was a bit hard on the bowler at that particular end. But O'Reilly swept this aside saying that it was good for the game. Fingleton regarded his old cobber thoughtfully for a moment. 'Quite right, Tiger,' he said, 'I can see you being the first to applaud the batsman who hit you into the front row – for six.'

4

These events took place in later years. The first fusion of the immense joint talent of Grimmett and O'Reilly was limited to the last two matches of the South African series in Australia in 1931-32. The South Africans were a very good side under the captaincy of 'Jock' Cameron but, on the plumb Australian pitches, they took a fair beating from a very powerful batting order, headed by Bradman at his very best. In five innings Bradman averaged 201.5, scoring 806 runs. The Australian bowling was not only better adapted to the conditions than that of their opponents, but of superb quality in the spin division. Ironmonger and Grimmett were more than enough to drive home the advantages that Bradman made for them. It was therefore a considerable compliment to O'Reilly, and a tribute to the discernment of the selectors that, when Ironmonger was not available. O'Reilly, in the early stages of his first season proper, was called upon. He took the field at Adelaide in January, 1931. (South Africa had, by then, lost the series in three straight matches.

Grimmett was very much the senior partner on this first meeting. Adelaide, his home ground, has always been regarded as a batsman's wicket, even by Australian standards, because of its rather easier pace. Possibly local knowledge played some part in Clarrie's wonderful haul of 14 wickets for 199 runs. South Africa did, in fact, put up a game fight in making 308 and 275, but went down by ten wickets. O'Reilly took four of the remaining wickets, two in each innings, for 155 runs, and, since one was Sandy Bell, a born number eleven, this was no wonderful record. As he bowled over 80 overs, it is clear that Bill Woodfull saw beyond these figures to the fact that he had acquired an altogether remarkable new bowler.

The final Test match was something of a freak and conveys no normal grounds for judgement. The pitch was a Melbourne 'sticky', possibly the ugliest proposition in the cricket world. South Africa made 36 and 45 and lost by an innings and 72 runs. Bert Ironmonger took 11 wickets for 24 so there wasn't much left for anyone else when Nash had taken 5 for 22. O'Reilly only got on in the second innings to take 3 for 19. He was luckier than some. Poor Clarrie, with 33 wickets in the first four matches, did not bowl a single ball in the match!

The partnership was now in being but not wholly established. Its next engagement led it into some rough waters, when Douglas Jardine fought his way through the tough series of 1932-33. The uproar which was aroused by 'bodyline' bowling has tended to obscure all other features of that season. An interesting one is that a strong English batting order split the newly formed axis. Grimmett was dropped after three matches in which he had taken but 5 wickets at 65 apiece. O'Reilly soldiered on and finished a losing series with the fine record of 27 wickets at just under 27 runs each.

Things were much better for the partnership in England in 1934. Clarrie was always a happy man on English pitches, with the softer turf to respond to his fingers and the humid air to aid his in-dip. These conditions were new to O'Reilly, but one look was enough to confirm his liking for them. I remember meeting Eddie Dawson one Sunday morning when he and his county had been bowled out by O'Reilly on his first official appearance. I asked him what he thought of this newcomer and he replied, simply and sincerely, 'He's the best I have ever seen'. It was a very fair judgement.

The partnership which had been riven asunder by the strength of England's batting in 1932–33 was reunited in the international plane at Trent Bridge in June, 1934. It was indeed a triumphant reunion, and worth studying in some detail as it marked the peak period which lasted until after the ensuing South African tour and final dissolution.

The Series of 1934 began in a somewhat delicate atmosphere for the wounds and resentment caused by 'bodyline' bowling were still close to the surface. But Larwood was now injured beyond recovery and Jardine had signified his intention of finishing his cricket relationship with Australia and Australians for good and all. The field was left to those on both sides determined that good relations should be restored: but they were, understandably perhaps, a little self-conscious in the early stages of the process.

The prospects of the actual play and its outcome were also uncertain for the departure of Larwood, perforce, and his partner Voce, in sympathy, had greatly levelled the chances. The Australian batting, untrammelled by this threat, was, again, just about as good as on the previous visit in 1930. The deciding factor could well be the penetrating power of O'Reilly and Grimmett combined, on English pitches. Their progress through the counties argued that this was likely to be powerful and sustained.

Trent Bridge, between the two world wars, provided, in good weather, a fine cricket pitch. It was one which at times resembled the Australians' home tracks, very true and very fast. It was already beginning to lose some of its pace in the 'thirties but was still much livelier than it became in post-second war years. Thus it was a good ground for a good bowler for, despite the scope it offered a stroke-playing batsman, it gave the ball plenty of pace and so afforded a good wide margin of length. Test match pitches were, of course, that much better than good county pitches, and so was this one on Friday, June the 8th.

Australia won the toss and batted through a dull first day,

weatherwise, to be out for 374 on the second afternoon. England had a new partner for Sutcliffe, Cyril Walters, a most elegant and enterprising opener. This pair saw the fast bowlers off after a short spell and addressed themselves to the major problem of the spinners. Walters was obviously troubled by Grimmett and out to his quick top spinner, l.b.w. at 45. Much now depended on Sutcliffe and Hammond and they found quite a battle on their hands. At an early stage in their acquaintance O'Reilly had discovered that his best line of attack against Hammond was down the leg-stump and here he always concentrated. Deprived of his galaxy of strokes to the off, Wally was inclined to chafe and fret, and O'Reilly nagged away with nary a mistake. When Wally was out at 102, things went none too well and Pat Hendren and George Geary alone took advantage of Sutcliffe's unwavering lead to save the follow on by 46. England were all out at three o'clock on Monday, 106 runs behind.

The first assessment of this leg-spin combination in its new environment was now possible. Between them Grimmett and O'Reilly had bowled 85 overs and 3 balls to take 9 wickets for 156 runs, Pataudi having fallen to Tim Wall. But for Hendren, a superb player of spin, and Geary's stubborn 'nous', the later batting would have disintegrated. It was a pretty good start.

When Australia declared, at 273 for 8, England wanted 280 runs to win and had four-and-three-quarter hours in which to get them. As, by now, the wicket was showing a few rather ominous cracks, and a few patches had roughed up, the prospects were never very good.

Once again Wall and MacCabe got the shine off in a short opening spell and Woodfull got his main artillery into action. They were not immediately successful for, although both got a good bit of turn, Walters and Sutcliffe got to 51 without apparent difficulty. At that score Sutcliffe edged O'Reilly into the slips. But then Hammond went quite comfortably: the fact that he was contained did not matter in the circumstances. Sadly, at 88 he overbalanced playing a long forward shot at Grimmett and was stumped. O'Reilly then bowled Walters, and Pataudi, who tried to hit Grimmett for six, was caught at mid-off. Hendren was caught in the slips off O'Reilly and five were out by tea-time. Leyland and Ames fought every inch but when Ames was bowled and Leyland caught at the wicket it was the end of effective resistance and Australia won with ten minutes to spare. This time the spinners had bettered their first innings record and had taken all ten between them. In that second innings they had bowled 88 overs and 4 balls for 93 runs. The match record was, Grimmett 8 for 130, O'Reilly 11 for 128.

Percy Fender was present throughout the match. No shrewder judge of the game in general, or spin bowling in particular, could be called upon for a general assessment of this wonderful performance. He wrote, 'It goes without saying that the bowling feats of Grimmett and O'Reilly overshadowed all else. I do not think that I have ever seen finer bowling, especially when it is remembered that they were slow bowlers and not on a wet wicket. That they got assistance from the wicket cannot be denied, but it is equally certain that they got all there was to be got out of that wicket, and kept going in a manner that earned the admiration of all who saw them. No fast bowlers could have done what they did, physical strength would not have permitted. It was only the fact that they were slow bowlers which allowed them to win that match for Australia, and the magnitude of their triumph was fitting to their ability.'

From their beanfeast of Nottingham the great duettists proceeded to their least successful engagement – at any rate in plain figures. The Lord's match will always be remembered for Verity's great bowling but, for the moment, we are concerned with that of the Australians.

England won the toss on a beautiful Lord's wicket but, at one stage on the first day, when half the side was out for 182, it seemed that the batting had failed. The supporting leg spinner, Chipperfield, was chiefly responsible for this as he had taken three of those wickets. O'Reilly had Walters caught in his short leg trap but Grimmett had not so far had a touch. At this point Leyland and Ames embarked on a massive partnership which added 129 for the sixth wicket which lasted into the second morning. When the English innings closed at 440 the bowling analyses disclosed the unusual fact that the partnership had taken no more than a couple of wickets between them, and that at a cost of 172 runs. Verity made such good use of the rain that followed that they had no opportunity of exploring what became a very helpful spinners' wicket.

At Manchester the pair found themselves in very similar case

WILLIAM JOSEPH O'REILLY 'The top-spinner O'Reilly spun rather more, and his "wrong 'un" he really buzzed. Every ball he bowled had a springing, bouncing quality which naturally grew more pronounced the greater the purchase afforded by the pitch'

RAY LINDWALL 'He has always insisted that the arm is merely the instrument for releasing the ball, and that the body does the main work in producing swing, pace and lift from the turf'

to that of Lords, a lost toss and a perfect, plumb wicket. Walters led England with such fluency that he had made 52 out of the first 68 runs scored when, with O'Reilly just about to be relieved, he fell into the famous short-leg trap, off a bouncing googly he had not quite covered. Now, of course, O'Reilly was not taken off. Bob Wyatt came in number three and was castled by his first ball. Wally Hammond glanced a four, survived the next ball and was clean bowled by the following one. This was a true reflection of O'Reilly's worth. Like all good men of action, generals or boxers, given an opening he would exploit it immediately and effectively. This was just about as rude and abrupt a turn of England's fortunes as could be imagined, and might have been the prelude to complete disaster. Hendren met the situation resolutely and Sutcliffe took as much of O'Reilly as he could, so danger was converted into triumph when Leyland added another century to his run of success. O'Reilly bowled heroically to take 7 wickets for 189. In the process, he dug such a hole with his left foot that Allen, trying to avoid it, bowled his famous 13-ball opening over for England. As Grimmett in the Lords and Old Trafford games had taken 2 wickets for 252, the partnership might again have been split – if he had been playing for the home side.

Leeds saw England saved by rain and the balance restored, for Grimmett got seven wickets, and O'Reilly five, out of the 15 which fell to Australian bowlers. At the Oval the splendid sight of Grimmett and O'Reilly in co-operation was seen for the last time. England were crushed and again the pair accounted for a dozen English batsmen. It was Frank Woolley's last Test match, and, hearing that he would play instead of the injured Hendren, Plum Warner prophesied he would be caught at short leg off O'Reilly. And so he was, when he had made 4. In the series O'Reilly took 28 wickets at 24.9 and Grimmett 25 at 26.7. Next best was Chipperfield with 5 at 44.

When Australia toured South Africa the following year the wickets were not very dissimilar from these of England in the 'thirties. That is to say, very well made and not so pacey as the Australian or West Indian. The South African batting was hardly as good as the English professional school, with Wyatt and Walters in support, and this disparity was especially noticeable when the opposition was the flight, spin and accuracy of the Australians. This time the partnership had a good aggressive lead

D

from Ernie McCormick at his fastest and the support of the rather erratic, but always dangerous, Fleetwood-Smith. Grimmett and O'Reilly hardly required either. With Fingleton and McCabe at the top of a fine batting array, they were always well on top of a courageous home side.

In the first match, at Durban, Grimmet took five and O'Reilly eight wickets to give Australia a nine wicket victory. At Johannesburg their haul was eleven in a drawn match, and at Cape Town Grimmett got ten to O'Reilly's five in an innings win. They got another fifteen in the fourth, an innings win at Johannesburg. The last match, at Durban, brought the same result and this time the pair took 17 wickets. But Grimmett claimed 13 of these and was, for once, the senior partner for the whole series. The figures read Grimmett 44 wickets at 14.59, O'Reilly 27 at 17. Perhaps Clarrie, hitherto unseen by most South African batsmen, was a bigger surprise packet than Bill and, also, he was comparatively a better bowler on this type of pitch whereas O'Reilly on the lightning fast or dusty pitch was generally regarded as the more dangerous.

Here the great association ends – surprisingly. As Clarrie had bowled so well in the South African series, it seems strange that this marked his last fling and so the end of the partners. When G. O. Allen led England in the surprising and exciting series of 1936–37, O'Reilly carried the burden of the spin attack. He was assisted by Frank Ward, a good honest spinner of the leg break, but not in the same class as Grimmett. There was also the tremendous but unpredictable left-handed wrist-spin of Fleetwood-Smith. Neither of these could substitute for the reliable, untiring and ever dangerous presence of Grimmett. He was still in good form, bowling well against the M.C.C. on three occasions and taking thirty wickets in Sheffield Shield cricket. Presumably his age of 44 was against him in a country where cricketers tend to retire young.

If his absence was noticeable in Australia it was, in the opinion of many judges, decisive in 1938 when Don Bradman brought his side to England. Old Grimmett may have been; but he could have been nursed for the big occasions (a policy he would have most fiercely resisted). In England his material worth would still have been considerable and the effect on the morale of his own side, and the opposing batsmen nigh incalculable. However, these are hypothetical speculations on a matter long since closed.

There was a point to which I said I would return to when considering the partnership as a whole. It is this. One of the fascinations of cricket is that there are as many ways of achieving a given point as possibly in a game of chess. The dismissal of batsmen by spinning the ball is a case in point. There are two extreme schools; the cavalier, represented by Mailey, and the calculating, exemplified by Grimmett. In between are a myriad of fine gradations.

The Mailey school will risk error and inaccuracy for the sake of enormous spin and the occasional unplayable – or at least wholly deceptive – ball. (In this discussion it is well to remember that all things are relative, and Mailey's 'inaccuracy' would be considered pretty tight bowling in terms of length and direction in humbler circles.) But the process, unless the bowler does produce a problem ball with fair frequency, is expensive and can defeat itself. The psychological balance is delicate and the striker who has just hit a couple of fours puts a confident bat to the good ball when it comes. Even if it defeats him, he is not necessarily out. Wright of Kent would have been one of the greatest of all bowlers had the art of bowling been confined to beating the bat. In practice he could bowl superbly for a fraction of the reward a rather greater degree of accuracy would have brought him.

The greatest and most effective bowlers have been extremely accurate. This is, I know, a bromide because it is a necessary ingredient of perfection. But Barnes, Bedser, Lindwall and some others have got as near to perfection in bowling as humans will. Grimmett and O'Reilly were both remarkably accurate. This was one great feature of the partnership. When they bowled together there was no suspension of the pressure for the batsman and, apart from a constant vigilant defence of their wickets, they had to *make* any runs which came their way. Again the batsman cramped and threatened does *not* put such a confident bat to the really penetrative ball if he has had no opportunity to assert himself. And if he was beaten by either of the comrades, the odds were that he was out, for they were always there or thereabouts, and so were their fielders – they could afford to be.

Grimmett and O'Reilly played together in 15 Test matches. In partnership they took 169 wickets, which means just over 11 per match. One remembers with regret that, in their second match, at Melbourne, when wickets were being almost given away, O'Reilly bowled but 9 overs and Grimmett none at all. In all they took 352 Test wickets between them, and every over either of them bowled was an object lesson and entertainment in itself.

As I have considered them as a whole and, as such, greater than the parts, a comparison of the absolute strength of their differing merits may be more than ever odious. It has, however, been a frequent one and so I shall once again make it. There can be no doubt that the majority of those qualified to judge would unhestitatingly put O'Reilly first and, indeed, first of all spin bowlers since World War I. That one or two thought Clarrie the better drew a rather back-handed compliment from one of the best qualified of all judges. I once remarked to Wally Hammond that a certain England cricketer thought Grimmett the better of the two. 'Maybe,' said Wally, 'He was never there long enough to see.'

FIVE

Ray Lindwall

by Ray Robinson

IN A spacecraft age we have grown used to speed, which is more than could be said of batsmen who faced Ray Lindwall. He is one of the few who have been able to demonstrate a truth not mentioned by Euclid: pace that shortens the distance between two given points.

None could ever say, paraphrasing 'My Fair Lady', that they had grown accustomed to his pace. Lindwall had more paces than they could keep up with. Between the extremes of a fearsome bouncer and a late out-swinger, he tried to keep batsmen guessing all the while. Hundreds guessed wrongly, if they had time to guess at all.

For a half-dozen years before Trueman trod a Test field, and while people were thinking Statham too fragile for such a part, Lindwall reigned as the world's No. 1 fast bowler, a matchwinner through a period of Australian dominance in international cricket. In those years before he passed his zenith he played in 36 Test matches, helped win 26 and was on the losing side only three times. Batsmen have since seen, if that is the word, the ball hurtle faster from the hands of Tyson and Hall - fractionally yet frighteningly faster - but their awesome presence did not confer on their teams such redoubtablity as the sides which had Lindwall from 1946 to 1952. With Keith Miller sharing the new ball and Sir Donald Bradman making hundreds in six of those Tests, it was like a conjunction of Mars, Jupiter and Saturn.

As one who saw Lindwall take his first Test wicket against England (Sir Leonard Hutton in 1946) and his last (Ron Swetman in 1959) and most of those against six countries in between, watching him deliver thousands of balls etched his exemplary approach on my memory as no other has done. The mind's eye sees a sandy-haired man of Swedish-Irish extraction enter the field in flannels that look looser than those worn by the other Australians, except the wicketkeeper. For a 13-stone man of 5ft. 11 in. his step is short, as if the least possible call is being made on muscle and sinew until all-out effort is needed. We see him swivelling his arms, marking time with high-raised knees and flexing his hamstrings by dragging each boot-heel up behind him. These activities are a continuation of loosening exercises begun in the dressing-room, where he has been jogging and touching his toes.

Sweater to umpire, and he turns at the windward end to pace out an 18-yard run-up, plus an extra step to make sure his take-off will be behind the bowling crease. He licks his first two fingers before placing them on the glossy ball. Anxiously, the striker watches him move from two walking steps into the thirteen running strides which form a model of accelerating approach. On the twelfth stride a high-leading left arm sets the line for a side-on delivery, with his back arched. Body momentum tows his arm over and a flick of the wrist propels the ball on its destructive way.

I believe the sight of that rhythmic approach brought one word to Sir Pelham Warner's lips, 'Poetry!' This reminds me of the way it impressed a more recent Lord's captain, J. J. Warr, who wrote in *The World of Cricket*, 'An incredibly smooth run-up, followed by a beautiful action, in which only the arm was lower than perfection decreed. The acceleration to the crease and the twinkling feet lent the illusion of his being pulled in on wheels by a hidden wire.' From one bowler to another this is a fine tribute, but there were times when Lindwall could have sighed for that hidden wire. His artistry might make it look almost effortless but his own lungs, limbs, groin and back told him differently. Once, as a Sydney film enthusiast, Leslie Barlow, showed Test pictures, I sat beside Ray, watching him bowl an eight-ball over on the screen. As he saw himself running up, he muttered, rather surprised, 'I don't *look* tired!'

Though he was influenced as a schoolboy by having seen Larwood bowl, Lindwall gathered speed more gradually and took one stride fewer. Instead of grounding his right boot parallel with the crease he pointed its plate-guarded toecap ahead. The plate scraped furrows across the line. His plunging follow-through carried him to the side of the pitch quickly, so he seldom caused complaints about roughening the playing surface.

He has always insisted that the arm is merely the instrument for releasing the ball, and that the body does the main work in producing swing, pace and lift from the turf. In his book, *Flying Stumps*, he tells how, soon after entering first-class cricket, he tried to act on well-meant advice that he should bring his right arm over at a higher angle than his habitual one, about 30 degrees from perpendicular. For him, it made a side-on body position uncomfortable so, after consulting the oracular O'Reilly, he stuck to his natural method. In fact, it brought advantages. Compared with the high-actioned Miller or Johnston at the other end, his bowling tended to skid rather than jump from the pitch. Whereas Miller's bouncer frequently sailed overhead, batsmen felt Lindwall's bumper was boring at their throats. Hutton, who ranked him first among bowlers he faced, found him hardest of all to sight, because the backdrop behind his hand was often the umpire, rising from a stoop.

October 3, 1921, was an inauspicious day for batsmen, birthday of Raymond Russell Lindwall at Mascot, between Botany Bay and Sydney Harbour. Australia and cricket everywhere owe a lot to W. J. O'Reilly having noticed his potential in schoolboys' street games. From Marist Brothers' College, Kogarah, Ray went on to the Brothers' High School, Darlinghurst. There he became captain of cricket and football and was champion athlete. Cricket's call was so strong that on Saturdays he used to play in a boys' team in the morning, then pedal his bicycle breathlessly to play in a men's match after lunch — all in a renowned sporting district, St George. A few weeks after he turned twenty, New South Wales sent him to Brisbane for his first inter-state match but a week later Japan's entry into the war ended first-class cricket in Australia.

At twenty-four Lindwall emerged from Army service in New Guinea and Pacific islands. Atebrin tablets gradually cleared up after-effects of tropical fevers but throughout his career he was plagued by dermatitis in a place subject to chafing. Before he had taken 15 wickets in first-class matches he scored 134 not out against Queensland in his fifth match, batting ninth and supported by skipper O'Reilly. The danger of a marked advance in the batting order was averted by ducks in Lindwall's next three games, so Providence was working in Australia's long-term interests and against those of batsmen in general.

His twelfth first-class match was a Test at Wellington, New Zealand, in 1946 and his first international victim was, appropriately, an opening batsman, W. M. Anderson. To further his unfolding career Ray quit his job in a Sydney engineer's office be-because he could not get time off to play and practise. Chicken-pox interrupted the new fast bowler's onslaughts on England's first post-war tour of Australia but on Adelaide Oval he electrified 31,000 watchers by taking three wickets in four balls. It was the first time an Australian crowd had seen such a feat against England. They were the last three, Bedser, Evans and Wright, but a dozen balls earlier he had caught-and-bowled Compton, 147. Presenting Lindwall with the ball, inscribed, the Governor of South Australia, Sir Willoughby Norrie, said, 'As an Englishman and a member of M.C.C., I trust that I will not be asked to repeat this type of celebration too often.' Only partly taking the hint, Lindwall mowed down seven for 63 in the first innings of the next Test in Sydney. In between, he sent a bail flying 143 feet 7 inches when he bowled Geffrey Noblet (South Australia). In taking seven for 38 in India's second innings in Adelaide in 1948 he dealt out four ducks.

After the 1947 change sanctioning delivery with the back foot lifted, provided part of it was behind the line, Lindwall was dismayed to find himself featured in a film. It showed that his right foot's drag across the crease carried him, sometimes, three feet past the stumps before the ball left his hand. (Others were to go further.) Next, a Sydney umpire, Cyril Wigzell, no-balled him for drag five times in three overs of an interstate match. There was nothing new about drag but Lindwall's speed made an issue of it. The resultant discussions caused his captain, Bradman, on the voyage to England in 1948 to advise Ray to concentrate on taking off even farther behind the crease and not to attempt full speed until umpires had scrutinized him in matches before the first Test. Before a battery of cameras at Worcester, the reluctant film star's take-off about 18 inches back was passed by umpires Dai Davies and Fred Root. Peace reigned ... at the bowler's end, that is. All through, English bastsmen felt that umpires were too lenient in their mark-back and should have doubled it, to three feet.

On the first afternoon of his first Test in England, Lindwall slipped on greasy turf at Trent Bridge delivering his last ball before tea. A pulled muscle in the right groin prevented him from bowling or fielding again in the match. Yet I was astonished to see him come in to bat midway through the game. Had Australia been in trouble, no doubt they'd have had to lock him in a lavatory to stop him but, as they were already 200 ahead, the decision to risk worse injury to the world's best fast bowler was incomprehensible. For nearly two hours Lindwall (averse to having a substitute) ran up and down. Sometimes he leaned over his bat or doubled up in pain. I still wonder whether, had his captain been a bowler, he would have scratched Lindwall's name off the batting order. That would have been the surest way to avoid the danger of losing the side's spearhead bowler for coming Tests and leaving him permanently susceptible to strains in this ticklish region. And what about Ray's own brain – the man Neville Cardus said had so many brains that it was a wonder he ever went in for fast bowling at all? After twelve days' rest, his warm-up ball in the Lord's Test pulled the groin muscle again, but less severely, and he manfully carried on. By the Manchester Test he was fit to bowl the swiftest overs he ever produced in England, in a dramatic clash with Compton and Edrich.

So on through post-war England Lindwall left a trail of shaken nerves and shattered stumps. This effect on dressing-room atmosphere can be judged from Yorkshire off-spinner Ellis Robinson's pantomime. Purporting to be next man in, Ellis would begin pouring a drink of ale. 'Who's bowling, Ray Lindwall?' he would ask anxiously, his trembling hand rattling the bottle against the glass. 'What? Colin McCool... ah!' and the rattling ceased as a steady hand finished the pouring.

But the rattling of stumps continued. It culminated in Ray's most deadly spell, 5 wickets for 8 runs in 49 balls after lunch in the Oval Test. In England's lowest-ever home total, 52, his innings figures were 6 for 20. With characteristic modesty, he discounted this by praising the catching of Hassett, Morris and Tallon and by saying most of the Englishmen expected the ball to fly from a length (the pitch having been made in rainy weather) whereas it went through at fairly uniform height. By taking 27 wickets in the five Tests (as did left-handed W. A. Johnston) he equalled E. A. McDonald's record for a fast bowler in a series in England.

As Lindwall left the Oval an acquaintance asked, 'Why wasn't somebody put on the other end who couldn't have taken a wicket and would have left them to you?' Lindwall: 'I wouldn't want to break a record that way. If that had been done for Grimmett he might have taken 39 wickets.' Praising Bradman for his captaincy, Ray said, 'Not once did Don keep me on for an extra over when I should have been given a rest.' One Australian has since bettered

27 wickets by a fast bowler – Graham McKenzie, 29 in 1964. A Barbadian, Charlie Griffith, took 32 in 1963 but batsmen expressed opinions about his delivery which could never have been passed about Lindwall.

To prepare for Ray in 1949, some South African batsmen tuned up against baseball pitchers. More groin trouble saved their having to face him at his fastest, and in the final Test of a one-sided rubber, a fast-medium bowler, Noblet, was given a chance in his place. Yet when he broke Mann's off stump at Johannesburg the jagged end stuck in the ground like a javelin. Earlier, at Cape Town, one Australian critic, who apparently thought Ray was having too much golf or drinking too much beer, or both, described him as a rather portly ghost of a once-great bowler. A few nights later Lindwall noticed the critic dancing, tapped him on the shoulder, asked could he take over his partner for the remainder of the foxtrot and added, 'Don't worry, I'm only a ghost.' Teammates jokingly called Ray 'Wraith' Lindwall but if he was a spectre to batsmen it was only metaphorically. His answer to the 'once-great' jibe: 45 Tests and 160 wickets later he set up a record total for an Australian bowler.

At a time when he was still chary of imposing full-stretch strain on his groin, Lindwall, then twenty-nine, was alongside the non-striker Dr George Thoms, in a pause in play at Melbourne. Thoms happened to say 'It is only a few years since I was sitting in the stand, watching you hurl them down at full speed.' An incautious remark, worth adding to the list of famous last words! Three balls later Thoms' stumps were scattered by a ball he scarcely saw. The departing Victorian's philosophic comment: 'As I walked away, it was no use yelling back that I hadn't meant it that way.'

By the time the West Indians, conquerors of England in 1950, left Australia in 1952 they could talk of little except the hostility of the fast attack by Lindwall, Miller and Johnston, who shared 64 wickets in the series. An umpire cautioned Miller for too many short-pitched balls in the first Test but two different umpires took no action in the fifth Test on a grassy Sydney wicket when the West Indians counted 25 bouncers in 40 balls by Lindwall to Everton Weekes. In six overs ten got up shoulder-high or head-high, while an extra fielder reinforced the standard Australian quota of three leg fieldsmen for fast bowling. Lindwall always contended that, as Weekes continued trying to hook the fliers –

against his captain's admonitions – he was justified in repeating them. With a few exceptions Australian writers and broadcasters condemned the frequency of the bumpers. O'Reilly believed that the umpires should have intervened, although most of the offending balls flew over the middle and off stumps and Law 46, defining intimidation, at that time specified balls 'at a batsman standing clear of his wicket'.

That match in 1952 and the Manchester instance in 1948 were the only times I saw Lindwall, in Tests, bounce three consecutive balls head-high to a batsman, but after surviving a fiery onslaught on a Sydney grasstop, Hassett, captaining Victoria, asked the umpire what was his definition of intimidation! Similar thoughts must have occurred to Hutton occasionally. Sometimes after ducking, he smiled – a smile like a man who has just escaped from under a moving train – and once Lindwall heard him mutter: 'Remember laad, one day we'll have a fasst bowler – and I hope that day isn't far off.'

Louder protests often came from crowds. When Walter Hadlee, after having retired hurt for six minutes, was knocked down by a second blow in the ribs Dunedin onlookers called, 'Take him off!' A bruised left-hander, Jack Smith, suggested photographing a Canterbury batsman in a crash helmet and sending it on to the next city as a hint on how to play Lindwall. Sydney barrackers rumbled when a bumper cannoned from the point of Tallon's shoulder to be caught at square-leg, leaving the Queenslander unable to bat in the second innings. An Adelaide crowd hooted Lindwall and Miller for bouncers after one of Ray's stunned Lance Duldig and caused him to retire hurt for twenty minutes. Probably the loudest demonstration against his bumpers came in a Melbourne match. After an over of short-pitched balls to Hassett ended with two head-high bumpers, a bouncer in Lindwall's next over struck Hassett on the chest. The little Victorian called 'What goes on?' and the bowler replied cryptically, 'I thought you'd like a few on the leg stump'. After another bumper dismissed Keith Stackpole the crowd's outcry caused the next batsman, E. A. Baker, to stand away from the wicket until the noise died down.

Twice his bumpers struck batsmen full in the face: Gordon Woolmer, who attempted a hook while batting for The Rest of N.S.W. in 1947, and opening batsman Jack Robertson, who tried to duck in Middlesex's second innings against the 1948 Australians. Neither took any further part in the match. Ray told me afterwards, 'The sight of their injuries, bruised and swollen, upset me so much I could hardly sleep. On a later visit to England, Robertson asked me to broadcast with him and told listeners I was one of his greatest friends. I'm not sure Jack's wife has forgiven me though.' The ball that gashed Compton between the eyes at Manchester glanced up from an attempted hook. No inventory was kept of the number of caps breaking the force of blows, much less of bruised ribs, thighs, elbows and sqrashed fingers. Ray did not seem to mind being nicknamed 'Killer', saying 'There's no sitting duck like a scared duck'.

Though his bumpers provoked boos on several grounds in England, they were usually accepted by West Indian crowds. In Georgetown we heard Lord Melody round off a calypso with these punch-lines:

>'Baul, Lindwahl, daun't be afraid!
>'Dem dat can't bat – break dey
> shaulder-blade!'

Development of his in-swinger in a season with Nelson in the Lancashire League preceded his 1953 tour. At thirty-two, he was still faster and kept a truer line than any quick bowler the Australians met in Britain. Compton's statement that a batsman could rarely get a sighter or leave a single ball alone was much more a compliment than a complaint.

Sponsors of a still-smaller ball invited the great bowler to Lord's to try it. By making it swing excessively either way, to pick off whichever stump he nominated, he caused the project to be dropped – thereby doing his kind a disservice, though everybody else thought it a good turn. That was in 1953 on his second tour of England. Soon afterward, in his thirty-ninth match in England, as he hauled off his sweater at Edgbaston the umpire asked him was he a right or left-hand bowler and, what's more, would he bowl over or around the wicket! News of this spread around the fieldsmen in one chortling flash. The explanation remained a mystery until a big leg-spinner, Douglas Ring, marked out his run-up. The same umpire asked the square-leg fielder, 'Is this Lindwall?' On discovering that he was talking to Lindwall, the umpire, a new man, apologised, 'Sorry, I thought you were a bigger fellow'.

Lindwall's drag, if we can forget his groin for a moment, was the touchiest thing about him. No-balling for this, when he felt it undeserved – as on his relatively slow ball – brought a few flushed-faced words with a couple of punctilious umpires and resulted in abrupt sweater-grabbing at the end of overs. Few other things ruffled his even temper.

His response to calls on his stamina near the end of the season deepened admiration for his fitness and team-spirit. For his eight wickets in the Leeds Test he bowled 89 overs, followed by a sustained spell of 90 minutes to break through Surrey's early batting. In a desperate attempt to prevent England regaining the Ashes at the Oval, he bowled 13 overs before lunch on the last day, 11 of them at the trot. Sir Donald called it a miracle that he came through the strain of the season without tearing a muscle. To his usual rôle of shock bowler he added the part of stock bowler in the final Test. To check scoring on the last day he resorted to a tight length and six on-side fielders. It demonstrated his versatility but went against his inclinations. He used to say that, if he bowled consistently at the leg stump, he believed he would be credited with more maiden overs but he doubted whether he would have derived any pleasure from bowling that way. As it was, his overall expense rate was 38 runs per 100 balls.

Lindwall's face has no sharp contours, but hours of concentration soon lined his brow. Through narrowed lids, his blue eyes kept batsmen under close inspection for weaknesses. So intent was his watch that fellow-players talking to him on the field got only monosyllabic answers, if that.

Occasionally he halted play in mid-over and waved deep fine-leg around 20 or 30 yards towards square, where a hook would often land. That made the striker think of a bumper, only to be taken aback by a yorker in his blockhole. Far from playing to the gallery, Lindwall played as if there was no gallery, only himself and the batsman who engaged his undivided attention. Yet his appealing was spectacular and athletic, emphasised by jumping and flinging both hands high as he whirled to face the umpire. It was likened to a Maori war dance, especially if the wicket was a prized one, that of Hutton, Compton, May, Weekes or Walcott. Then we would see him finish by leaning forward and patting both knees, not so much gloating as showing satisfaction and relief at the overthrow of such a respected opponent. His yorker was aimed as accurately as Russia's Pacific rocket. Miller, known for picking up the bat with a masterful backswing, came in to face him and, on a hunch, raised the bat-end only a foot from his boots. Along came a fast yorker but the bat came down just in time. Before he walked back for the next ball, Lindwall called up the pitch 'Can't you lift the bat now?'

After one of their early encounters Lindwall drove Hutton from Sydney Cricket Ground to the English team's city hotel. Sir Leonard recalled years afterwards 'We didn't speak a word to each other, apart from saying "Good night!" By actions in the middle, we had told each other a good deal about each other's play. What was there to say after all that? Besides, we did not want to give away any more secrets.' They had never had a real talk when, years later, Hutton travelled by the same train as the Australians after a Test in England. So Len strolled over and said, 'Ah'd like to have a little chat, Ray.' For a moment he was nonplussed when Lindwall came back with, 'I've seen enough of you on the field without wanting your company off it,' but it was only a joke and, instead of a little chat, they were soon conversing freely.

However word-bound he might seem in midfield, Ray's tongue had no trouble loosening at a party. Perhaps the huskiness of his voice came from wind blowing down his throat as he ran up to deliver more than 40,000 balls in first-class cricket!

The late-to-bed, late-to-rise timetable of touring Australians suited him. He and his regular room-mate, Miller, often ordered breakfast trays for 10 a.m. That enabled them to appear just in time to catch a car to the ground. The pair always divided their hotel bills fifty-fifty and scooped up roughly half any cash they left on tables. Once Miller found a crumpled slip of paper, 'Lindy £10.' He asked, 'Do I owe you a tenner or do you owe me?' Neither could remember, so they called it square and tore up the slip. When Ray appeared in a Brylcreem advertisement, peacefully holding a bat for Miller to sign, his tawny hair hardly rivalled the gloss of Keith's – but then, it wasn't combed so frequently. The Queen honoured each with an M.B.E., Miller while on his last playing tour of England and Lindwall nine years later.

After Lindwall's first experience of playing before television cameras, a woman lip-reader wrote asking him to moderate his language on the field. She had seen him, so she said, make remarks after an umpire rejected his leg-before-wicket appeal. In apologising, Ray added a rider that such vocabulary was unbecoming to a gentlewoman!

After he yorked Reg Simpson, first ball, in a Brisbane Test a writer asked how long Simpson batted. The scorer: 'One minute.' When Ray heard of that, his dry comment was, 'slowest ball I ever bowled!'

Tyson and Statham ousted him from the centre of the stage in 1954. The contrast in speed was heightened because Lindwall, 33, was affected by hepatitis (inflammation of the liver) which kept him below his best during three years of enforced teetotalism. In the final Test against Hutton's team, with his total at 99 wickets, Ray was mortified by seeing two good catchers, Davidson and Johnson, drop chances. The sight struck a compassionate spot, hitherto unsuspected, in Bailey's make-up. Knowing that England's innings was about to be closed, Trevor stepped outside the last ball before tea and was bowled behind his legs. As the players walked off through separate gates, a double ovation recognized the bowler's record and Bailey's gesture.

Though most cricket followers are primarily interested in batting, when the Australians reached Jamaica for their first Test tour of the Caribbean the men West Indians seemed most eager to see were Lindwall and Miller. An Australian critic heralded their arrival by writing that his country's fast attack was in 'an advanced state of disintegration', a kind of aspersion they enjoyed bowling out with never a blink of their none-too-serious blue eyes. Instead of falling to bits themselves, they disintegrated the West Indians' batting. The pair topped the wicket-taking in the rubber with 20 wickets each, though grassless pitches wore the shine off the ball in a few overs and the atmosphere was unfavourable to swing in all islands except Trinidad. I can still picture them toiling under scorching sun, their lips blistered as its pitiless rays fried the sweat trickling down their faces. Despite a recurrence of hepatitis, Lindwall still had enough speed, on occasions, to do such things as splinter the top of a stump in bowling Collie Smith in the Bridgetown Test. (Among the witnesses was a teenager named Wesley Hall.)

Rather than disappoint a Grenada crowd, Lindwall bowled

against Windward Isles in spite of a carbuncle on his right forefinger. The Windward captain, Dr Rupert Japal, and the umpires willingly approved his bowling with a plaster on the painful finger. Ray took two wickets. After Windward Isles scored 274, six Australians were out for 60 when Lindwall joined captain Ian Johnson. The finger had become so painful that his skipper told him in Australianese he could give it away. Lindwall: 'Give it away! What are you talking about? If we get out, Australia will have to follow-on. I'm going to stay. Will you be with me?' He batted more than two hours to make top score, 68, in an 113 stand with Johnson that preserved national honour. His skipper would not allow him to take any further part in the match, which was drawn.

Cricket and his family life were intertwined. Ray was visiting Brisbane to play in a Sheffield Shield match when he first met a blonde model, Peggy Robinson, whom he married after eight months' courtship. New South Wales selectors put a black mark against their State's name when they left him out of what would have been his farewell match before his switch to Queensland, where he bought a $9,000 home at Mitchelton Heights. A son, Raymond Robert, was born in Manchester while the father was Nelson's professional. A daughter, Carolyn Gail, arrived in Brisbane while Ray was on his way home from the West Indies.

Apart from his groin and other over-stretched muscles, he shared another weakness common to bowlers of all paces: being sure he had a batsman plumb leg-before-wicket when the umpire could see otherwise. Yet his essential fair-mindedness came through in such remarks as one he made when asked about the umpiring in the West Indies in 1955: 'The only two really bad decisions were both in Australia's favour.' In a Sydney Test Lindwall dived for a low return from Statham but shook his head to indicate his attempt had failed. Yet the nearest fieldsmen appealed and were sure his hand made the catch. In a Leeds Test a head-high legside full-toss to May was swung downward behind square, where a sprawling Lindwall rolled over with the ball and held it up, claiming a catch. May naturally waited until the appeal was upheld. When his partner, Washbrook, came off at the day's end he asked Peter 'Were you out?' May: 'I couldn't tell whether it carried to him but, knowing Lindwall . . .'

When Ray said, 'Fast bowling is the toughest job in sport –

tougher even than Rugby League,' he was speaking from experience, as he won State selection as a full-back before he gave up football to conserve his physical assets for cricket. If bowling strained a muscle anywhere he showed boundless faith in two masseurs with the gift in their hands, and would travel 500 or 600 miles to receive instant healing from Saunders of Melbourne or Roberts of Newcastle. Finding golf a relaxation but insufficient to keep him fit enough, he ran roads like a training boxer, before each season, and exercised like a gymnast. He could raise and lower his 180 lb. frame in thirty press-ups on end without falling on his face. His back – so often a worry to fast bowlers – is still a picture of rippling muscle. No shoulder-blade or knob of backbone is visible. A narrow valley down this muscular expanse shows where his spine is.

Stretching exercises between seasons gradually toughened his groin, preparing the muscles for the stress of his extended delivery stride, though they still niggled at him occasionally. He so built up his body and stamina that he continued to be one of the world's front-rank bowlers at an age when most fast bowlers have given out in the knees, feet, back or bellows.

Never complacent, he constantly strove to keep his action fully efficient. Long after he scaled the pinnacle of fame Ray confessed, 'When nobody is looking, I'm always bowling stones at trees and posts'. All through, inner wisdom made him know better than to wear himself out trying to flog speed out of a paceless pitch. On such turf he would bowl within himself and rely on his other skills. Observing this from Sydney's Hill one day, a man kept calling, 'Well bowled, Grimmett! '

On his third tour of Britain, 1956, Lindwall missed the only fast wicket, Lord's, because of a strain, and had only 100 overs in the rubber, for seven wickets, on tracks which unduly favoured spin. His total of Test wickets stood at 199 when he slipped on a greasy patch at the Oval and pulled a thigh muscle. On Karachi National Stadium's mat his 200th victim, Zulfiqar Ahmed, edged a catch into Langley's gloves. Lindwall always had the support of wicketkeepers with dexterity to gladden a bowler's heart – Tallon, Langley, Grout – and if injuries put them out the capable hands of Saggers, Maddocks and Jarman kept the glovework at a high standard. After Ray bowled Australia to victory over India with seven for 43, a Madras linotype operator unwittingly gave a comical twist to his newspaper's praise: 'Lindwall bowled with accuracy and skill never seen before in this part of the country. This was bowling of the highest order, revealing the class he is imbibed with.' A thirst-provoking thought for a man who had hardly tasted an alcoholic beverage for three years!

While such things were going on, newspaper articles about the tour of England appeared under his name before the side returned home. For this breach of tour contract the Australian Board of Control docked £50 from his good-conduct bonus. A plea that the infringement was a syndication error beyond his control failed to absolve him, though it probably averted a heavier penalty like the £100 imposed on Miller. The offenders were in distinguished company, as another player penalised by this authority had been Bradman in 1930.

Lindwall's £1,300 fee for six months with Nelson set a new high level for the Lancashire League, yet his cricket career did not reward him on the same scale as other front-rank players, such as Bradman and Hassett, or as Miller and Benaud, whose retirements at the height of fame were timed to capitalize on their renown. No doubt Ray missed similar openings by continuing longer in the game. From Testimonial funds he received the equivalent of £1,525 sterling.

The name Lindwall was missing from the Australian XI for more than two years. Yet he was determined not to accept eclipse as permanent. To tone up leg muscles he pedalled a stationary training cycle on the lawn of his home for half an hour each morning for three months – the equivalent of hundreds of miles. He nicknamed the bike 'Ching', because his wife, watching him pedalling without getting anywhere, sang 'Slow Boat to China'. It was she who, when he almost lost heart, encouraged him to press on with his training. He could run up a nearby hill which necessitated changing gear in his car. When his out-swinger was not going away as it should, he diagnosed the cause as a fault that had crept into his delivery, making it less side-on. So he rigged up a rope and pulley at home to help exercises restore his left arm to the desired elevation.

At last he convinced watching selectors that he should be recalled by taking 7 wickets for 92 off 29 overs for Queensland in heat that touched 110 degrees on Adelaide Oval, scene of the next Test against May's Englishmen. Selection meant that, as a veteran of 37, with experience in 55 Tests, he had to play under a fourth captain, nine years his junior – Richie Benaud in his first season as skipper. A likely source of embarrassment, you might think, but sportsmanship and team spirit enabled them to accept the situation with reciprocal grace. In a side containing three pacemen Lindwall found his right hand sharing the new ball with Davidson's left hand, on his merits. He dismissed an opening batsmen in each innings and Cowdrey's wicket left him needing one more to overtake Grimmett as heaviest wicket-taker for Australia. Within the limits – but only just – of the duty of beating England, his new skipper gave him full opportunity. Every time Benaud put him on to bowl Adelaide Oval's bars would empty as men swarmed out to witness the historic event. The cohorts of well-wishers were unable to jostle Destiny.

With his first ball of the Melbourne Test, Lindwall had Bailey caught by Davidson – at fourth slip, mind you. When he bowled Bailey for 0 in England's second innings he turned to wave to the women guests' enclosure, where Peggy waved back; she had waited four days to see him lift the record. In the hotel that evening Bailey, looking at the menu, said, 'Roast duckling – that would be appropriate'. Passing his chair at that moment Lindwall put a hand on his shoulder and said, 'I didn't do it, Trevor – it must have hit something.'

His influence on the game once prompted me to say Lindwall changed the look of international cricket and the expression on a thousand batsmen's faces. His example reshaped Test attacks – other countries' besides his own. No fast bowler had lasted long enough in Test cricket to reach 100 wickets until he proved it could be done, at the age of 33 in his 26th Test. As Roger Bannister's breaking the four-minute barrier opened the way for milers in several lands, so Lindwall's breaking the 100-wicket barrier has been followed by fast bowlers of four countries: Miller, Johnston, Davidson and McKenzie of Australia, Statham, Trueman and Bailey of England, Adcock and Pollock of South Africa and Hall of West Indies. Proliferation, if you like.

Twenty months after his hundredth victim, Lindwall's 52nd Test brought his 200th wicket – a total which had been attained by only two men in cricket history, Grimmett, a slow bowler with a six-step approach (216 wickets in 37 Tests) and Bedser, England's medium-pace genius who lumbered up nine strides to confound 236 batsmen in 51 Tests. Following the Lindwall trail past 200, Statham went on to 245 wickets in 69 Tests and Trueman stormed along to 301 in 65, despite selectors' readiness to leave him out. Though he never rivalled Lindwall's accuracy (did he try to?) Freddie could bowl one ball better than Ray, his fast in-cutter.

Up to his 150th wicket Lindwall's average striking rate was a wicket in every 52 balls. Though he continued pace bowling until four months past 38, still respected if no longer dreaded, this did not dilute his career rate past 60 balls a wicket. So Test wickets fell to him with quicker frequency than they did to his confederate pacemen, Miller and Johnston, or to Statham, Adcock or Heine, Davidson or McKenzie. Two advantages over his successors were that, for several years, new balls nestled in his fingers more frequently than bowlers have known since 1955 and there was no front-foot rule to peg dragging bowlers back until three years after he retired.

He was the first fast bowler to use an umbrella field in Test cricket, at the instigation of Miller, who had already tried it and liked it in interstate matches after his old Services XI team-mate, Keith Carmody, had introduced it in Western Australia. We saw third-man and long-leg called up into an eight-strong catching arc, mid-on brought in a few yards from the striker and only one fielder, Harvey at cover, left in a run-saving position. In 48 innings in which Lindwall and Miller began Australia's bowling against England only nine times did both partners survive until the total reached 50; six times they went on to a century partnership. In half those 48 innings the first wicket tumbled for fewer than 20.

Lindwall's last four Tests in Pakistan and India lifted his total to 228 wickets, taken with 13,666 balls in 61 Tests. Among the 228 were 145 in the first six of the batting order, 67 of them opening batsmen. He bowled 103 men in Test matches and skittled 14 Englishmen for 0. Twelves times he captured at least half the wickets in a Test innings.

His total of 789 wickets in 224 games is the highest by any Australian fast bowler in first-class matches for his country, State teams and in Test trials and testimonial games. McDonald, most destructive of all speedmen from Down Under, disposed of most of his 1,365 victims for Lancashire in county cricket. Some of F. R. Spofforth's 840 wickets were taken for Derbyshire, and the leading Australian cricket statistician of his day, E. H. M. Baillie, made his total 767 in 136 matches of the kind in which Lindwall took 789. I calculate that Ray ran more than 415 miles to bowling creases and walked a similar distance between balls.

Had he been only half so good a bowler – or a quarter – he could have been a valuable all-rounder for any side. He was the seventh player in Test annals to make 1,000 runs as well as take 100 wickets, and went on to top 1,500 runs and hold 26 catches. In addition to two Test hundreds, he scored the swiftest half-century in Anglo-Australian matches in 45 blazing minutes at Lord's in 1953. His Melbourne 100 off English bowling in 1946 came in 113 minutes, aided by three chances. In Barbados he climbed out of a vinegar-and-water bath (a precaution against stiffness) to raise a ton in 145 minutes. Nervous about the first ball, Lindwall always received it the same way, packing up half-back behind his bat. Once the ignominy of first-ball dismissal was escaped, he drove with frequency and power that left cover and mid-off standing. Once he opened New South Wales' innings and topped the score. When leaky coverings resulted in a sticky wicket – a rarity in Adelaide – South Australian captain Phil Ridings sent N.S.W. in. As Skipper Miller wanted to hold his best batsmen back, in the hope of the track improving, Lindwall and wicketkeeper Geoff Trueman volunteered to go in first. Ray scored 70 of a losing total, 148. One May day at Fenner's in 1956 he raced to 100 in 106 minutes against Cambridge. Yet at Karachi in 1959 he was Australia's last man in and made 23 of 38 for the last wicket with Davidson.

Only one chance came for Lindwall to captain his country in a Test – at Bombay in 1956. Weakened by injuries and illness, it was a scratch side but you'd never have thought so, seeing the way they responded to his inspiringly aggressive captaincy in the heat. The Brabourne Stadium wicket was too good to permit a finish. As Queensland skipper from 1955 to 1960 his out-cricket leadership could not have been bettered but in direction of the batting he sometimes seemed more scared of losing wickets than would have been expected from his own play.

Lindwall achieved his bowling triumphs against batsmen as good as we have seen, on wickets usually better than, say, Boycott has known. Before surfaces favoured seam and cut, bowlers had to beat batsmen in the air, chiefly, by change of course and change of pace. Lindwall was a master of both, with control that has yet to be equalled at such speed. To the end, he usually completed an eight-ball over inside four minutes – a credit to himself and a reflection on others.

He was 44 when a fall in a single-wicket match severely damaged his right knee. After an operation next day to avert the risk of permanent stiffness, he partnered his wife in a florist's business in Brisbane. For such a warrior on the cricket field, a life amid sheaves, petals and blooms may seem rather incongruous until we remember how often he cut down the flower of England's batting.

SIX

Alec Bedser
by John Woodcock

ALEC VICTOR BEDSER was more than a great bowler. He was, and is, a very dear man, abounding in integrity, softened by a gentle nature, and inspired by an unshakable desire to give of his best. It is always a pleasure therefore, to meet him, and a privilege to write about him.

If, in this one paragraph, I have made him sound a paragon, he will be embarrassed. He has no time for flattery, or for things fanciful, or for praise that might sound too fulsome. His success, both on the cricket field and now in business, has been based, he will say, on those simple virtues which the young of today tend to look upon as being 'square' or old-fashioned.

On the most recent of his many visits to Australia, in 1962–63, this difference in outlook between Alec and the modern generation was there for all to see. He travelled as assistant to the Manager, the Duke of Norfolk. Besides being in charge of the net profits of the tour as well as the net practices, he liked to bowl at Tex Dexter's team whenever he could, and he had, to some extent, to familiarise the Earl Marshal with managerial routine. It was a full-time job. Yet at Adelaide, on successive mornings, Alec was up by six o'clock searching his accounts for a few shillings that had gone astray. To him, the players tended to take their responsibilities too lightly. To them, Alec was seeking perfection in an imperfect world. The two, while being incompatible, were the best of friends.

This then is the man who, with his great strength and wonderful natural rhythm, carried England's hopes of bowling Australia out in the years after the Second World War. He and his twin brother, Eric, joined the Surrey staff in 1938. When the time came to enlist with the Royal Air Force in 1939 they had each played twice for Surrey. Within a few weeks of their coming back from the war, in 1946, Alec was being compared with Maurice Tate. By 1948 he was a household name, and the comparison with Tate still stands, these two and Sydney Barnes being the greatest of all medium-paced bowlers.

Between 1912 and 1937 Tate took 2,783 first-class wickets, 155 of them for England. Between 1939 and 1960 Bedser took 1,924 wickets, of which 236 were for England. For the best part of 50 years one or the other was pounding in to bowl in his outsize boots, the ball sounding like the crack of a whip as it hit the wicketkeeper's gloves. If the work of these two in their cricketing years could be collected and piled up around them in visible shape, what a vast mound there would be! And each carried unrepining the heavy harness of labour – in all weathers, winter and summer. They were idols in their own country and immensely popular abroad. There was something about them (though I can speak only of Bedser at first hand) which told you that if victory was possible no effort would be spared to achieve it.

You always knew when Alec was in the mood. His head would start to bob about as he came in from his mark. Sometimes the earth would seem to shake. No one was safe on such days as these. Bradman described the ball from Bedser that bowled him at Adelaide in the Fourth Test match in 1946–47 as the best ever to take his wicket. 'It was delivered,' wrote the Don, 'on the off stump, swung very late to hit the pitch on the leg stump, and then came back to hit the middle and off... There is no doubt in my mind that I found Bedser harder to play than Tate, especially in England in 1948.' After qualifying this assessment by saying how his own advancing years had caused his reactions to slow down by the time he met Bedser, Bradman paid both men the same tribute. 'They were magnificent bowlers, delightful personalities and ornaments to the game.'

Arthur Morris, one of the finest of all left-handers and a prolific scorer for Australia after the war, was so harassed by Bedser, particularly on the leg stump, that in the end he conceded him a telling psychological advantage. In the 21 Test matches in which they were opposed to one another, Morris lost his wicket 18 times to Bedser. Against Australia alone, Bedser took 104 wickets, a number surpassed only by Barnes with 106 and Wilfred Rhodes with 109. Barnes's wickets came in 20 Tests, Rhodes's in 41, Bedser's in 21; and the majority of Bedser's were taken at a time when only Doug Wright, the most mercurial of bowlers, could offer him any high-class support. Between 1946 and 1953, whenever England came near to beating Australia Bedser played the leading part.

Happily, before his powers began to wane he saw to it that

England regained the Ashes for the first time after the war. Not all the methods employed by England to overcome Australia in 1953 were entirely creditable. Had they bowled at Leeds as they would have thought the Australians, in similar circumstances, should have bowled at them, they would have lost the fourth Test. Instead they bowled altogether too wide. But when, after England's victory at the Oval, the final count was taken, it was Bedser's bowling that had won the series. His 39 wickets in the 5 Tests was the highpoint of his career. Yet by the Christmas of 1954 he was in eclipse, the end having come with a suddenness that was sad to those who saw it.

The beginnings, back at Woking in the 'thirties, had not been especially auspicious, there being no promising history of cricket in the Bedser family nor obvious athleticism about either Alec or his brother. It is to be remembered when reading the Bedser story and picturing Alec in war and peace, that his identical twin was almost invariably in his shadow. The first time they were separated was when Alec went to Australia in 1946, by when they were twenty-eight, and even then it was only a few weeks before some kind friend paid for Eric to set off in pursuit of Alec. In middle age it has become easier to tell one from the other. The overs that he bowled took a toll of Alec and have made him thinner in the face than Eric.

But in the slight whine of their speech, and in the things they say and think the two are still remarkably alike. Often one of them will start a sentence with a slight stammer and leave the other to end it, also with a slight stammer. Doug Insole, Essex captain and England selector, tells the story of how he was batting at the Oval against Surrey in 1950 soon after Alan Rae, the West Indian opener, had made a century in the Lord's Test match. After finishing an over Alec remarked to Insole: 'Takes a bit of digging out, this Rae.' As Alec moved away to his place in the field Eric came in from deep third man. Going up to Doug, Eric promptly said: 'Takes a bit of digging out, this Rae.'

They have always worn the same clothes and hit the golf ball the same distance with the same club from matching bags. I remember playing with them at Worplesdon when, off the first tee, they both took a Number 2 wood. Both skied their drives a little, after addressing the ball in the same deliberate manner and swinging the club through the same rather restricted arc. Both balls ended on the fairway, eggs in the same nest. In case I have conveyed the wrong impression, they have single figure handicaps and win a great many more matches than they lose.

As a cricketer Eric held a regular place in the Surrey side from 1946 until 1961. Although, like Alec, a seamer when he joined Surrey, the demand was for an off-spinner, and it was in this capacity, and as an opening batsman who later went down the order, that Eric made his mark. He would probably have done the double of 1,000 runs and 100 wickets in the season with some regularity for one of the lesser first-class counties. As it was, he gave Surrey staunch service and graduated to a Test Trial in 1950, the game in which Laker took eight wickets for two runs on what *Wisden* described, somewhat euphemistically, as 'Bradford's sporting turf'. Eric Bedser's 30 in the second innings was the highest score made in either innings for the Rest. In 9 overs Alec had not succeeded in taking his brother's wicket.

Credit for persuading the Bedsers to leave the solicitor's office in which they were working and try their luck with Surrey belongs to Alan Peach, an old Surrey player who had a Cricket School in Woking. They had both been making runs and taking wickets for the local club, and since boyhood their main interest in life had been games. By the time the war was over they were big, strapping fellows 6 feet 4 inches tall and weighing 15 stone.

Alec was thus built for work. Not for nothing was a racehorse named after him! His shoulders and arms were massive and his action was a fine one. In parts it was classical, with the weight thrown well back on the right foot at the start of the final swing, the shoulders giving full momentum to the delivery, and the follow-through as near to perfection as you are likely to see. From illness and injury he seemed immune, until, on his last and least successful tour to Australia, he went down with a bad attack of shingles. For most of the time early bed and early rising, no smoking, a healthy amount of beer and regular golf kept him fit.

With the resumption of first-class cricket in 1946 Alec was soon among the wickets. In his first match for Surrey he took 6 for 14 in M.C.C.'s second innings, and by the end of May he had ensured his selection for England. In his first Test, against India, he took 11 for 145. He followed this with 11 for 93 in the second Test at Lord's so that within a few weeks of returning to the Oval in no little trepidation he could look forward to spending the winter of 1946-47 in Australia. Like some great galleon, he was set on his course, a symbol of reliability, the same in fair weather and foul.

England's side on that first post-war tour to Australia was potentially full of runs. Of the batsmen, Hutton, Compton, Edrich and Washbrook were approaching their peak and, although he failed in the Tests, Hammond was still capable of great things. The bowling leaned too heavily on Bedser and Wright. Australia, led by Bradman, discovered the nucleus of a magnificent side, and one that over the years was to present England's bowlers, of whom Bedser was the mainstay, with so much toil and sweat. Morris, Miller, Lindwall, Tallon, Johnston and Johnson all came to maturity in 1946-47. Neil Harvey followed soon afterwards, and both Hassett and Barnes were left from the Australian side of 1938. It was against such an array of talent that Bedser pursued his Test career. Like Tate in the 'twenties, Alec was often to play a lone hand.

In his three Test matches against India, Bedser had taken 24 wickets and paid a song for them. As soon as he got to Australia he found the going very different. His 16 wickets cost him 54 runs apiece. He knew for the first time what it was like to come in at the end of a hot day with feet on fire and head singing. In the first Test Australia made 645. In the second at Sydney they declared at 659 for 8. Bradman scored 187 and 234 in the two games, and at Sydney he and Barnes added 405 for Australia's fifth wicket. Bedser, having taken 2 for 154 at Brisbane, had 1 for 169 at Sydney. By the end of the third Test at Melbourne his first 9 wickets against Australia had cost him 598 runs. He was learning, in the hard way, a lesson which he never forgot – that length and perseverance are prerequisites for success against Australia.

In his book *Farewell to Cricket*, Bradman wrote of Bedser's bowling at Brisbane 'Under extremely trying conditions Bedser in particular put up a grand exhibition of bowling. Seldom can anyone have bowled so well to have finished with such poor figures, or have seen so many possible chances go astray. Even a touch of the sun (which caused Bedser to leave the ground) did not subdue his spirit. He returned to the field and caused us to defend with all the skill we could muster.' Bradman doubted whether, in that series, Bedser ever completely recovered from 'the terrible gruelling he received in that stifling heat'. Certainly in 1947 his bowling showed a temporary decline. He was dropped from the England side after playing in the first two Tests against South Africa. Butler, Copson, Gladwin and Edrich opened the bowling in turn, and when M.C.C. went to the West Indies in the winter of 1947–48 Bedser stayed at home to rest. West Indians were, in fact, never to get a glimpse of Bedser's bowling in their own islands, for in 1953–54, when M.C.C. went next, he again declined an invitation.

In 1948 the Australians were in England for the first time for 10 years. Their side, led again by Bradman, was one of the finest they have ever fielded. They won the series by four to none: and of all their first-class games they won 23 out of 31, 15 of them by an innings and were never beaten. They were the last of the really high-scoring Australian teams, seven of their batsmen averaging over 50 and ten of them collecting 47 hundreds between them. For England Bedser was the chief attacker, though he had to work like a Trojan for his wickets. The 18 that he took included Bradman's four times in a row. As he had also accounted for the great man in the second innings of the last Test at Sydney in 1946–47 Bedser had his wicket in five successive Test innings. Bradman's scores were 68, 138, 0, 38 and 89.

It was now, in the evening of his career, that Bradman seemed to show just a flicker of fallibilty. He had not done so since the body-line of Larwood and Voce in 1932–33. In 1948 Bedser made a habit of having him caught at backward short leg off the inswinger. Before the war Bradman was seldom attacked on the leg stump. Tate, for one, bowled mainly on or outside his off-stump. Bedser chose a different line, and Bradman found himself glancing uppishly to a position round the corner some eight or ten yards from the bat, where Hutton used to lie in wait.

Bradman was less concerned by what was only a comparative failure (he averaged 72 in the Test matches) than by the principle that he saw to be involved. He came out strongly against 'this modern habit of bowling medium pace inswingers to a modified leg-field', not for any personal reason but because he thought its general effect on the game itself was bad. 'I refused to be chained down into inactivity by an obvious plan,' he wrote, 'and paid the penalty with my eyes open.'

In 1948–49 Bedser made his only playing visit to South Africa,

ALEC VICTOR BEDSER 'You always knew when Alec was in the mood. His head would start to bob about as he came in from his mark. Sometimes the earth would seem to shake. No one was safe on such days as these'

JIM LAKER 'Few, especially among his opponents, would dispute that Jim Laker was the finest off-spinner of his own, or probably any, period'

with George Mann's side. 'Wherever they went,' said *Wisden*, 'on their 10,000 mile tour from the Cape to Victoria Falls and back, M.C.C. attracted unprecedented crowds for cricket in South Africa.' The game was still being played in that wonderful aura of relief and bonhomie that existed for a while after the war. South Africa were less than a genuinely formidable side; M.C.C., with Compton, Hutton and Washbrook in full bloom, could afford, more often than not, to play relaxed and carefree cricket. England won two of the five Tests, both narrowly, and in gaining swift inroads into South Africa's batting England were indebted largely to Alec, who was always more likely than anyone to dismiss the best batsmen. All but five of his wickets in first-class matches came in the upper half of the order, and he suffered badly from chances missed in the slips.

As a batsman, Bedser, in this series with South Africa, figured in one of the most exciting of all Test finishes. With three balls of the first Test left, any of four results was possible. England, with two wickets to fall, needed two runs to win, and off the sixth ball of the last over a single from Bedser levelled the scores. Gladwin missed the seventh ball, whereupon these two stalwarts, neither of them noticeably swift of foot, decided, whatever happened, to attempt a run off the eighth and last ball. It was a leg-bye that did the trick for England, with batsmen and fielders scampering and pounding in all directions.

As Alec came to bear an increasing burden as a bowler, his batting declined. To begin with he was scarcely inferior to Eric. A straight hitter with a good solid punch his finest hour was against Australia at Leeds in 1948, when, after going in as nightwatchman, he made 79 and shared a third wicket partnership of 155 with Bill Edrich. This is one of the moments of Alec's career which he most likes to dwell upon. To hear him talk of it, with a swell of pride, you would think that had he not held back at one of Ian Johnson's off-breaks in deference to the luncheon interval and been caught and bowled, he would have broken all manner of records. His highest score and solitary hundred was 126, for Surrey against Somerset at Taunton. All told he made 5,735 runs at an average of 14.94.

As for his fielding, he was happiest in the gully or at slip, where he was within conversational range of Godfrey Evans or, more often, of Arthur McIntyre, both of whom always stood up to him when he was bowling. He bestowed upon McIntyre his most openhearted friendship. There was a coterie in the Surrey club in those days, composed of long-serving players, who must have seemed to the apprentices like a barrier to progress. As in Yorkshire, the young players had often to wait a long time for their chance.

Alec's catching, when he got a hand to the ball, was of the safest. He was not quick, which was hardly surprising, but those hands were as huge as the jaws of a whale, as anyone will know who had them grip his shoulders in a good-natured vice, if there is such a thing. At mid-off or mid-on Alec's movements were stately. He was the battleship in the fleet. For England Cyril Washbrook, and for Surrey Bernard Constable, were the destroyers who did some of Alec's fetching and carrying for him.

But to return to Bedser the bowler. In 1949, hampered by a strained hip joint, he was rested from England's team in the second Test match against New Zealand before returning to take 7 wickets in the third Test at the Oval. Between April and September he got through his usual thousand overs, and a winter at home was a welcome rest before the arrival in England of the first of the all-conquering West Indian sides in 1950. This was the year in which Surrey won their first championship since 1914. Bedser's contribution was in the shape of 90 wickets at 20 runs apiece.

Against West Indies Bedser again bore the brunt of the bowling, though to less than his usual effect. For an England side plagued by injury and desperately short of good bowling, West Indies were far too strong. Worrell, Walcott, Weekes, Ramadhin and Valentine so dominated the summer that when England left for Australia in the September of 1950 they were given, rightly as it proved, small chance of regaining the Ashes. Alec, whose 11 wickets against West Indies had cost him 34 runs each, was considered by a number of eminent judges to have passed his prime, due not least to age (he was thirty-two) and overwork. They pointed to his arm having dropped and to his step having lost its spring. And they were wrong, as any Australian could have told them a few months later.

Against another fine Australian side, now selected rather than captained by Bradman, England were wonderfully served by Hutton and Bedser, with Freddie Brown, the captain, and Trevor Bailey giving Bedser some of the bowling support he needed. It was from the time of this series in Australia until the end of 1953 that Bedser was at his best. There was an occasion at Melbourne in the second Test when he was almost unplayable. In England, where the ball moves about more eagerly, he had days of terrible havoc. Those who played against them both credited Bedser with a better inswinger than Tate and Tate with the more dangerous outswinger. But in Bedser's armoury the most lethal weapon was the leg-cutter, the equivalent of a fast leg-break that would pitch on the leg stump and miss the off. When this was really 'going' no one could cope with it. In addition Bedser's change of pace was often deceptive.

In Australia Bedser's finest performance was at Melbourne on December 22, 1950, just as Barnes's had been on the same ground on December 30, 1911. England lost the toss on a pitch which had been covered for some days from persistent rain. Though true, it was fast, and it encouraged movement off the seam as well as late swing. Bedser must have been delighted with the conditions, and no one at the Melbourne Cricket Ground that morning had ever seen finer bowling than his. Morris was soon in the bag, and Harvey, already a brilliant player, was beaten five times in two overs by the giant who tormented him. Evans's wicket-keeping had to be seen to be believed that day, his taking down the leg side of Bedser's in-swingers being, even by his own standards, marvellously assured. It was an inspiration to bowlers and fielders alike. By evening Australia had been bowled out for 194; in their second innings they made only 181; and yet England lost the match by 28 runs.

This was the first time I had been on tour with Bedser and the first time therefore that I had seen how much the Australians liked him. No matter where he went he was the same to everyone – genuine, loyal and completely without airs. His disappointment in defeat (England lost the first four tests before winning the last) was philosophical, though he would always say what he thought. England's batsmen were generally the target of his wry, rather laconic, and active sense of humour. Active it always was. In the autumn of 1967 I received a News Sheet from a Cricket Society in Sussex in which the author said how pleased they had been to welcome Alec Bedser, who *'as a scratch golfer'* had been able to talk authoritatively about two games. Knowing that his handicap was, in fact, eight, I sent the cutting to Alec with an 'aggrieved' note to say how disillusioned I was to have discovered in this improbable way that he had been playing golf against me off a false mark. In future, I added, I would know to claim the full allowance. His reply was on a good length: 'Dear Splinter, as usual the information transmitted to the public is incorrect! So please, once again, take everything you read with a pinch of salt! P.S. I started the game too soon. £3,000 a year!'

Alec's own earnings from cricket were quite inconsistent with the great efforts that he put into it. Nonetheless he enjoyed a bumper benefit of £12,866, a sum surpassed only by Washbrook, and more important than this, he made a great host of friends. He was always the first to go to the Australian dressing-room for his glass of beer at the end of a day's play, and even in 1950–51 and 1953, when he was giving their batsmen such a drubbing in the middle, there was always a warm welcome for him. To Alec, cricket was a game to be played and enjoyed as such. Never for him the cold war or the smouldering recrimination. David Sheppard, in his book *Parson's Pitch*, tells of feeling nervous in the England dressing-room before his first Test match against West Indies. Bedser was lying face down on the table, having his back massaged. 'Would you like a knock? I'll come and bowl at you,' he said. It was typical of Alec's thoughtfulness.

England's victory at Melbourne in the fifth Test in 1950–51, their first over Australia since before the war, was hewn to a large extent by Bedser. His 10 wickets for 105 runs in 42.3 overs was a fitting climax to the best of his overseas tours. With another 30 Test wickets coming his way in 1951, against South Africa, he brought his total in a year to 62. Against South Africa he bowled a little matter of 275 overs. At Nottingham in the first Test he had 6 for 37 in South Africa's second innings; in the third Test at Old Trafford he took 7 for 58 and 5 for 54; and when winter came he was fast approaching the record number of Test wickets, held for England by S. F. Barnes with 189 and for Australia by C. V. Grimmett with 216.

Being a proud workman Bedser took a pride in his many records. He was fortunate, no doubt, that during the fifties English pitches were being prepared to favour bowlers. Word came from Lord's that they were to be made more 'sporting', and nowhere were these instructions interpreted more literally than at the Oval. To make matters worse for batsmen the ball seemed never to lose its sheen across that lush green outfield. Bedser, Loader, Laker and Lock were immensely formidable. One county after another was mown down, and no touring side tackled Surrey without fearing for their reputation. In 1956 they defeated the Australians – the first county to do so for 44 years – and from 1952 to 1958 they won the Championship. All the while Bedser was adding to his great collection of wickets.

In 1952 he took 102 at 15.51 apiece; in 1954, 89 at 13.30; in 1955, 117 at 16.92. In the early years of Surrey's supremacy he was frequently away on Test duty, as were Laker and Lock, but in the Surrey notes for the season of 1952 *Wisden* recorded that Bedser 'at times looked better than ever'. For England that year he was taking another 20 wickets against India for only 279 runs, to bring his Test total to 182.

In the first Test of the following year, with the Australians back in England for a thrilling series, Bedser's magnificent form enabled him to surpass Barnes's record. Since then Trueman has overtaken Bedser's final total, as have Richie Benaud and Brian Statham. But in 1953 Bedser was the name on everyone's lips. The rubber with Australia yielded him his last great international triumph. England, under the professional captaincy of Len Hutton, regained the Ashes for the first time since 1938, and Bedser's bowling was the greatest single factor in their victory.

No one from either country had ever taken 39 wickets in a series before. At Nottingham Bedser had 7 for 55 and 7 for 44. At Lord's he took 5 for 105, at Old Trafford 5 for 115 and 2 for 14. At Headingley it became 6 for 95 and at the Oval, in Australia's first innings, his figures were 3 for 88. There was no holding him. His cut and swerve and control were too much for Hassett's side, as they would have been for perhaps any other. For the last time in his career England's efforts centred round Bedser. He bowled, by prescriptive right, the opening over of an Australian innings, and he was generally the one to finish it off. In the first Test when he took 14 wickets (only Laker, Rhodes and Verity have ever taken more in a match against Australia) the Australian score at the end of a restricted first day was 157 for 3. Bedser's figures at the time were 25–12–26–3. That was the measure of his worth to England and of his hold over Australia. Time has not dimmed the memory of that summer which reached its climax at the Oval when the whole country seemed to stand still as England scored the last few runs to regain the Ashes. Bedser that night was the same unaffected fellow he had always been. Nothing ever went to his head, which was part of his charm.

One of the most remarkable aspects of this famous summer was the fact that Alec was 35. He could bowl so well only because he had kept himself so fit; and yet by the end of the following year he had had to give way to youth. I remember it well. At Brisbane in November, 1954, England took such a hammering – by an innings and 154 runs – that there seemed little future for them. Alec's return of one for 131 in 37 overs gave no indication of the ill-luck that he suffered in the way of dropped catches. Between this debacle at the Woolloongabba and the second Test at the Sydney Cricket Ground, Bedser took a well-deserved rest in the bush, this having been planned for some time to coincide with the State game against Victoria. Tyson played in the match at Melbourne and found a pitch to his liking, on which, in Victoria's first innings, he took 6 for 68. Had Bedser played he might, I suppose, have taken 6 for 30. A wild horse at the start of the tour, Tyson was lassooed and now broken into work. After endless discussions the selectors picked him for Sydney, in preference to Bedser, and he went on to play, with Statham, the vital part in retaining the Ashes.

Poor Alec! On the day before the match rumour had it that he was going to be left out, a rumour that he got wind of himself. In his heart of hearts he realised, I think, that he had not fully thrown off the effects of a nasty attack of shingles earlier in the tour. Yet like the great warrior that he was, he was keen to play. For some reason known only to Hutton, Alec was left to read of his omission when England's team was pinned on the dressing-room door. And he was obliged to spend the rest of that day and all the next watching a duel fought out on a pitch that might have been made to suit him.

Australians used to say that had Alec played England would have won this second Test more easily than they did. But there was no denying that Australia were demoralised by the sheer speed of Tyson, who for the remainder of the series was an automatic choice. One Test appearance against South Africa in 1955 – when injuries were prevalent – was Bedser's last. It was poignant, somehow, to watch his eclipse in Australia; and yet it is with nothing but pleasure that one reflects on his achievements as a whole.

His days as an England bowler over, Bedser's last seasons were devoted exclusively to Surrey. He soon became vice-captain to Peter May, who was England's captain at the time, and whenever he had charge of the county side he brought great determination to the job. May had great affection for Bedser – a feeling which was readily reciprocated by Alec who never failed to recognise a class player when he saw one – and in 1957 Bedser was May's own recommendation to the Surrey committee to be his deputy. It proved, in the words of *Wisden*, 'a wise and happy choice, Bedser's wide experience, deep technical knowledge, shrewdness and willingness to encourage the new members earning him a new stature in English cricket'. May made no secret of his respect for Alec's advice and judgement. 'He and I run the show together,' he would say, 'including the selection.'

Alec had always been a powerful advocate of a professional's right to the captaincy of a county side. 'I cannot be persuaded to believe that an amateur at 22 can do the job any better than a young professional... Discipline is necessary of course, particularly where young players are concerned, but I feel sure that players would become used to being captained by their professional colleagues and grow up in that atmosphere.' What he hoped for has now, to all intents and purposes, come to pass. Although the distinction between amateur and professional has been abolished the majority of county captains are appointed today, for better or worse, from what would have been the professional side of the fence. Unfortunately they are not all of Bedser's calibre.

Be that as it may, Bedser was determined to prove his point when he assumed his authority at the Oval. Fully recovered from the shingles that had beset him at Perth three years before, he captained Surrey twelve times in 1957 and had a large share in their sixth successive Championship which was gained by the enormous margin of 94 points. In 1958 Alec went down with pneumonia on the eve of the season and played only a minor rôle in another of Surrey's years. His bag of 48 wickets was the lowest of his career. In 1959, when Surrey were toppled at last, the rising cost of his wickets indicated that the old zip had gone, and at the end of the 1960 season, when Surrey were no longer serious Championship contenders, Alec hung up his boots. In his last game he led Surrey to victory by an innings over Glamorgan, after having taken 5 for 25 in their first innings. His figures were 20.3–9–25–5 and he was at the start of his 43rd year.

Between 1946, when he was having doubts about his cricketing future, and 1960 he took 14 wickets in a match twice, 13 once, and 12 twice. As soon as he retired he was appointed to numerous committees, including Surrey's, and before long he became an England selector. He also continued to play cricket for good causes. Though the old joints began to creak he continued for some time to practise what he preached by bowling a length. Late in 1962 Alec played in a Charity game in Brisbane. Keeping wicket was Wesley Hall, the great West Indian bowler, who knew what he was doing, having begun life as a wicketkeeper for his club side in Barbados. As often happens in Queensland at that time of year there was some damp in the wicket, and Alec's leg cutter was spitting like a rattlesnake. Wes's profession of admiration (he said he had seen nothing like it before) and Alec's acceptance of it were equally charming.

As a selector Bedser found nothing too much trouble and no journey too long. In business he and Eric continued to be first into the office. For his services to cricket he was awarded the O.B.E. He became an Honorary Member of M.C.C. and Captain of the County Cricketers Golfing Society. He wrote no book that darkened his own name by challenging the good name of others. And he remained, as everyone knew he would, unspoilt by fame.

SEVEN

Jim Laker
by John Arlott

'I S'POSE IF I wuz to think every ball, they'd never get a run.' Thus, with more perception than modesty, William Lillywhite, the first master of round-arm bowling, put his finger on the nub of the matter – the power of the thinking bowler. Many bowlers may be roughly equal in the mechanics of their craft, but the truly great have always been distinguished by thought. There have been off-spinners – though few – who spun the ball as much as Jim Laker; some of them had comparable control. But no one has ever matched him in those two departments and had, also, such a quality of intelligence.

If Jim Laker is to be credited with one outstanding attribute, it must be that of intelligence: and not merely intelligence, but *applied* intelligence. There have been thoughtful off-spin bowlers in recent years whose ideas often led them to cling stubbornly to uneconomic methods of attack. From Jim Laker's intelligence, however, stemmed other assets: it produced, importantly, the observation, judgement and flexibility which enabled him so rapidly to assess changing circumstances and change his method to suit them. Tom Goddard was, to an entire generation, the personification of the off-spinner: Laker himself had an immense admiration for him. But Goddard was essentially an attacking bowler. On responsive pitches he was a killer; but often he persisted in attacking on an unhelpful pitch or against a batsman who had his measure when, in his and his side's interests, it would have been better to apply the curbs of restrictive length, line and fielding-setting. This was a mistake Jim Laker hardly ever made. Given the right conditions – or, as in his great triumph at Old Trafford, even *half*-right conditions – he could be a destroyer. On the other hand, when the pitch favoured batsmen, he could bowl so tightly as to confine the best of them, and fret them into self-destroying error. He did so, with sustained effect – and perhaps most surprisingly – in the West Indies, in 1947–48 at the very outset of his career, when he was quite raw; and, as is more often remembered, in 1958–59, when the Australian batsmen, remembering their indignities of 1956, were grimly bent on revenge on their own pitches.

Few, especially among his opponents, would dispute that Jim Laker was the finest off-spinner of his own, or probably any, period. It was not simple coincidence that the years of his maturity were also a period of sustained success for both his county and his country. Yet it would do him less than justice to overlook the fact that he produced some of his most sustained and skilful bowling in losing sides. Both his figures and his style argued that he was unusually mature at the very outset of his first-class career and still unquestionably a great bowler at its end.

Memory will always recall him, very English-looking, six feet tall, firmly built, fair-haired, fresh-faced, quiet in demeanour, coming up to the bowler's end, with his shoulders hunched, cap at a jaunty angle. He moved to his bowling mark at a constabular stroll and, with the laconic air of one with his tongue in his cheek, pattered along a run of artfully-varied, short strides. Then, wrist and arm cocked, from a good, sideways-on beginning, he swung through a model, high delivery-arc into the positive follow-through which generated so much spin and life.

Jim – James Charles – Laker is a Yorkshireman; he was born at Frizinghall, Bradford, on 9th February, 1922. Almost invariably we find that great performers in any field grew up in an encouraging environment – a senior member of the family has been an enthusiast, if not an exceptional executant, so that it has been part of the background of the growing child. So far as Jim Laker knows, however, no member of his family before him had ever seriously handled a cricket bat or ball. His father was an outstanding runner, but he died in 1924 and, from the age of two, the boy, youngest of five children – he had four sisters – was brought up by his mother. His mother encouraged him to play, but the cricket of his formative years was limited to street-corner and waste-ground games, or the matches of a school at which sport was not seriously regarded. Here, though, it should be mentioned that his headmaster has followed the career of his only Test-cricketer-pupil with faithful interest.

It might seem tempting to suggest that Laker's ability was purely instinctive but, in light of his character, it is likelier that, finding the game attractive, he applied himself to it with greater acumen than most boys of his age. Certainly his development was rapid and, by the time he was fifteen, he was playing cricket for Saltaire High School on Saturday morning and in the first – Bradford League – eleven of Saltaire in the afternoon. At this time he was primarily a batsman and went in number four for Saltaire. His bowling was less esteemed. Like most strong, fit, young men at some time or another, he bowled as fast as he could and, though he had occasional success – he once took six wickets for no runs in a school match – he asserts that he has never, either then or at any other time, been able to swing even a new ball.

His batting talent did not pass unnoticed. The strength of Yorkshire cricket is only partly due to the size of the county's population. Its real power lies in the fact that a boy is more likely to play cricket – and plenty of it – in Yorkshire than in any other county; and, if he has merit, it is more likely to be observed, cherished, developed – and reported to the county authorities – there than anywhere else in England. At sixteen, within a few weeks of leaving school, the young Laker was summoned to the Yorkshire nets at Headingley. There he formed an enduring respect for his coach, Ben Wilson who, before the first World War, had been a plodding opening batsman for Yorkshire and later became a wise and helpful coach at St Peter's School, York, and at Harrow.

Laker was by no means alone as a promising young batsman under the county's observation: Willie Watson, Harry Halliday, Vic Wilson and Johnnie Lawrence (who later joined Somerset) were among his near-contemporaries and while the first two, slightly senior, gained places in the Yorkshire Second XI, the three younger players progressed no further than the nets in prewar years.

This did not seriously disappoint young Jim Laker. Like most Yorkshire lads, he enjoyed the game: but he had no thought of making it his career. When he left school he was content to become a clerk in Barclays Bank. So it was largely for pleasure that he returned to the Yorkshire nets in 1939. There he occasionally bowled off-breaks sufficiently well to impress Ben Wilson, who advised him on grip and method. He remained, however, largely a batsman. In 1940 he was top of the Saltaire batting averages for all matches but, in a side able, in War time, to call on several Test bowlers, he bowled little.

Before another English cricket season began he joined the R.A.O.C. as a National Serviceman and was posted to North Africa, so that it was not until after El Alamein, in 1943, that, on leave-trips to Cairo, he had the chance to play any cricket. At that time there were enough first-class cricketers in that theatre of war to produce some distinguished play in the good conditions at

Gezira. It was there, in the nets, that Laker had his first experience of matting wickets. To his delight he found his off-break turned far and quickly on the mat. Bowling it in matches against strong opposition, he achieved such performances as 8 for 36 against Gezira Sports Club which made a marked impression on his opponents. Peter Smith, of Essex, was among them and he pressed Laker to consider joining that county when the war was over. The gossip that leaked back to cricket circles in England linked him with the New Zealander, Bert Sutcliffe, as players unknown before the war who looked good enough to measure up to first-class standards in the post-war game. He cherishes, too, having been chosen to play for the M.E.F. at soccer.

On his return to England he was posted to London to await demobilisation and, since his mother had died during the war, he felt no compulsion to return to Yorkshire: so, when he left the Army and the Bank posted him to South London, he settled there contentedly enough, and joined the local Catford cricket club. A series of those mild accidents which have shaped so many careers took him to Surrey. Peter Smith had remembered him and ensured that he was offered a trial for Essex. He accepted, but in one of his last Army matches, immediately before his Essex date, he spun his index finger raw for the first of many times, and had to withdraw. Soon afterwards he played for Catford against a full-strength Nottinghamshire side in a Sunday benefit match when Andy Kempton – then President of Catford and captain of Surrey Second XI – was watching. Kempton who, coincidentally, also recommended Tony Lock to his county, passed Laker's name to The Oval. Invited there for a trial, he bowled so impressively to the county's captain-elect, Errol Holmes, that he was forthwith offered a contract.

Still not yet committed nor fully convinced, he played for Surrey against a strong Combined Services side at The Oval. His first wicket was that of Don Kenyon, caught at the wicket playing for the turn of a ball that ran on: he took Kenyon's and Bernard Constable's wickets in each innings and had 6 for 121 in the match. He had measured his wit and technique against established players and, in his heart, knew he was good enough for the county game. Yorkshire, approached by Surrey, remembered him as the useful Saltaire batsman of 1939: but they were not short of batsmen and consented to his release: Surrey specially registered him at once.

He played in two more non-Championship matches at the end of the 1946 season. But Surrey in 1947 with a seam-bowling strength chosen from Alec Bedser, Alf Gover, Stuart Surridge, Jack Parker and Eddie Watts, and two spinners – Stan Squires and Eric Bedser – both worth a thousand runs, had no pressing need for another slow bowler. So far as a vacancy existed, it was contested by Tony Lock and John McMahon, both slow left-arm and, therefore, affording greater contrast to Eric Bedser than a second off-spinner.

So, by the end of June 1947, Laker had appeared in only two Championship fixtures. In July, although he did not play regularly, he bowled usefully in both Yorkshire matches and achieved the best figures thus far in his short career – 7 for 94 in Surrey's narrow win over Essex – which won him a regular team-place.

The county cricket grapevine is a strong growth, and reports on the new Surrey bowlers travelled quickly. It was said, with some respect, that the batsman at the non-striker's end heard the ball hum with spin as it left Laker's hand.

This was the year of Edrich and Compton, when Middlesex massacred the bowling of county after county and, winning the toss against Surrey, they batted first on a good Lord's wicket. This was a searching examination for Laker, for both Compton and Edrich were merciless punishers of off-spin: in the Middlesex innings of 462 for 7 declared, he bowled more overs – 32 – than any other Surrey bowler and, for 105 runs took the wickets of Sid Brown and Denis Compton, and had two catches dropped. As if to demonstrate the excellence of the pitch, he made top score – 33 not out – of the first Surrey innings and the highest-but-one – 60 – in the second. He had surmounted the steepest hurdle: he was given his county cap. Although he played in only 14 of Surrey's Championship matches in 1947, he was top of their bowling averages with 66 wickets at 16.65 (Alf Gover was second with 109 at 24.09); and he was invited to play for Sir Pelham Warner's XI against the South of England – in effect a Trial match – in the Hastings Festival. In the first innings he bowled 22 overs and took 2 for 73: in the second, 33.2 overs for six wickets – including Denis Compton's, *and* a hat trick – for 109.

As a result, after virtually only two months in first-class cricket, he was chosen to go to the West Indies that winter. That was perhaps the most unnecessarily depressing tour in English cricket history. The initial error lay in selection which omitted Yardley, Hutton, Edrich, Compton, Bedser, Washbrook, Gibb and Wright. Hutton was flown out later to replace the injured Brookes; but this was a laughable force to pit against a West Indian batting strength of Weekes, Worrell, Walcott, Goddard and Stollmeyer on their own pitches. Allen, the captain, tore a muscle while skipping on board ship on the way out while, of the remaining bowlers, Butler, who broke down three times and bowled only forty overs in Tests, Cranston, Tremlett, Ikin and Howorth were all out of action for varying periods and Laker, despite painfully damaged stomach muscles, bowled more overs and took more wickets – 18 – than anyone else in Tests, and was the most successful bowler, in aggregate and average, for all first-class matches of the tour. He played, too, a courageous innings of 55 in the second Test when he took the leading part in a new record last wicket stand for England against West Indies. *Wisden* reported that 'undoubtedly he was the find of the tour'.

He returned, still with less than a full season's cricket behind him, an accepted England player. This was high success, and perhaps only he realised how far he was still short of the standard he recognized. This was the year of Bradman's unbeaten Australians. They met Surrey early in May and, on a good first-day wicket, Barnes, Bradman and Hassett made centuries in a total of 632: Laker's only success – the inconsiderable wicket of Bill Johnston – cost him 137 runs: it was the worst analysis of his career. A fortnight later he played in the Test rehearsal, M.C.C. *v.* Australians. Once more the tourists' batting rolled mightily: they scored 552. Miller mounted a powerful attack on Laker and, at one point on the second morning after a shower had reduced the pace of the pitch, he and Johnson between them hit him over the short, legside boundary for nine sixes. If he had wavered he would have been overwhelmed but he maintained his length and line and took the wickets of both Miller (163) and Ian Johnson (80).

So he went into his first Test against Australia, at Trent Bridge, and marked it with the highest score of the English first innings – a calmly made 63 in a total of 165 – before he took the wickets of Morris, Barnes and – sweet revenge – Miller, beaten by a ball which moved away from, instead of in to, the bat, for 0 – and Ian Johnson. At Lord's he barely bowled in the first innings: and in the second he might have had the wickets of both Barnes and Morris in his first over, but ended with 2 for 111 and lost his place for Old Trafford.

He came back on his native ground at Headingley where he suffered the first real setback of his career. When Yardley declared on the last day and left Australia to make 404 to win in 345 minutes, England had the chance to win. The pitch had crumbled and, if it offered greater opportunity to the wrist-spinner than the finger-spinner, Laker, nevertheless, several times made the ball both lift and turn. Certainly, Bradman was missed three times off him: but the Laker of three or four years later would not have allowed the left hander, Morris, to score a century or Australia to make 404 for three. Perhaps the tension and importance of the occasion threw him off balance; and if we remember that Laker was still only playing his first full season of cricket, that is at least understandable. Moreover, Bradman on the kill presented an insoluble problem to most bowlers of his time and Morris, riding the luck of his finest season, was a commanding hitter of the ball. The fact remains that Laker, probably in trying to overcome the slowness of the pitch, lost control of both length and line – as he had never done under pressure in the M.C.C.–Australians match at Lord's – and, since he was Yardley's main strategic weapon, he carried the burden of the general – and especially the selectors' – disappointment at the English defeat.

He was not quickly forgiven. On figures he remained one of the leading spinners in the country. In 1950, too, he achieved a unique bowling analysis. In the Test Trial at Bradford, Yardley, captain of England, put The Rest in to bat on a rain-damaged wicket. Several of the original selections had dropped out and four of the first five batsmen were still undergraduates, three of them at Cambridge, where they had enjoyed the amiable wickets of Fenners. Nothing, however, can detract from the quality of Laker's bowling.

There were few spectators at Bradford on that first morning and when I sat down on the pavilion balcony I certainly did not expect to see the most statistically remarkable performance ever recorded in first-class cricket. After Trevor Bailey had taken the wicket of David Sheppard, Laker came on at the Pavilion end. Characteristically, he had assessed the wicket before he began to bowl. It was a 'sticky' and he employed the correct technique, bowling round the wicket and never indulging in the higher curves of flight which might allow a batsman to move down the pitch to him. But, bowling through a tight arc, he varied his degree of spin, creating doubt in the mind not only of the batsman facing him, but also the man at the other end – and those watching from the pavilion – by making the occasional ball, though apparently spun as sharply as its predecessor, flick away outside the off stump. From behind his arm it was apparent that he never bowled a loose ball: his line was meticulously precise, and his combination of length and turn was such that he often both compelled and defeated a full-stretch forward defensive stroke. He took three wickets before a run was scored from him (that came when he gave Eric Bedser 'one off the mark' – a slow full-toss which Eric pushed gently to his brother Alec) and four more before he was edged for another single. Altogether, he bowled fourteen overs, twelve of them maidens and took eight wickets for two runs. It made a farce of the game as a Test Trial, but it showed Laker in the ruthless, destroying vein that was to distinguish many of his subsequent performances.

He had not made the South African tour of 1948–49, played in only one Test of 1949; and, despite his performance in the Test Trial, he appeared only once against the 1950 West Indians: and he was not picked for Australia in 1950–51. In 1951 he was top of the English bowling averages for the series with South Africa and decided the fifth Test, which won the rubber, with ten wickets and an eminently sensible innings in the tense and precarious final stages: but he played in only two of the five Tests: and, although he played in all four Tests in 1952 against India in England, that was a fast bowlers' series and he bowled only 90 overs.

He was not picked for the first two Tests against Australia in 1953 but he came in at Manchester where, on the last day, when play was resumed after rain with a draw apparently certain, he began, and Wardle continued, the Australian collapse which first revealed their vulnerability to the turning ball and reduced them to 35 for 8 wickets by the end of the match. At Headingley, when Australia seemed set to win easily, he played the fast bowling of Miller and Lindwall with cool efficiency for almost two hours to make 48 and, as it proved, to save the game. At The Oval he made the initial break-through in the second Australian innings, bowled steadily in face of a late onslaught and, with

Lock, set England in the position to win the match and the rubber with it.

He went to the West Indies in the following winter and bowled with fine stamina and control in the last four of the five Tests of that hard-fought and, eventually, tied rubber. Then, however, he was chosen only for the first Test against Pakistan; was not taken to Australia in 1954-55 and, against South Africa in the following summer, was not picked until the last Test when, once more, he (seven wickets) and Lock (eight) won the match and the rubber on their home pitch at The Oval.

Nothing in Jim Laker's career is more remarkable than his relatively small number of Test appearances. He did not make a gradual way into representative cricket: indeed, he played in every match of his first rubber – against the West Indies in 1947-48 – and in all but one (when he was unfit) of his last, in Australia in 1958-59. For a decade he was the finest off-spinner in the world yet, between his first and last Tests, England played 99 matches and he took part in only 46 of them. In those games he took 193 wickets: only three other England bowlers – Trueman, Statham and Bedser, all of whom played in more Tests – have exceeded that aggregate. Moreover, Laker's average is lower than that of any other England bowler of modern times with even a remotely comparable number of wickets and, since the First World War, only Trueman, Bedser and Tyson have bettered his striking rate of four a match.

During his thirteen years with Surrey they were once joint-Champions and won the title for seven consecutive years, from 1952 to 1958: that sequence ended when, for the first time in a full season of play, Jim Laker failed to take a hundred wickets.

With Alec Bedser, Peter Loader and his fellow spinner, Tony Lock, he completed one of the finest all-purpose attacking units any county has ever possessed and the support, at different times and in varying degrees, of Stuart Surridge, Eric Bedser, Tom Clark, Ken Barrington and Jack McMahon gave the side the asset, outstandingly valuable in English conditions, of finishing matches quickly.

Popular memory and the record books will always recall 1956 as his greatest season: yet it is doubtful if he was a better bowler then than in several previous years or at least a couple afterwards. In that summer he had some pitches and some luck to help him:

but he might have been equally successful in any other year after he perfected his technique and before the damage to his spinning finger began to affect his bowling.

In that year Jim Laker was 34, with a half-mannerised hint of stiffness in his movements, but fit in the quite unique way that first-class cricketers are fit. A famous athlete is supposed to have said that English cricketers were unfit. It may well be true that few of them could sprint a quarter-mile under pressure in any considerable time. But we may wonder how many fully-trained runners, encumbered by flannels and cricket boots, could open the bowling, flat out, at half-past-eleven in the morning, and, at intervals of fielding for six hours, come back after lunch, in mid-afternoon and at the end of the day, and, each time, bowl five or six accurate, high-speed overs; or, as Laker often did, bowl for two or three hours in the heat of a tropical afternoon with such undeviating steadiness as to pin down the finest attacking batsmen in the world.

Physically economical of energy, he walked back six paces to his mark and came in up a short-stepping 'run' which he deliberately varied from ball to ball, changing its pace or number of steps, a subtlety which made it difficult for the batsman to time his approach. He gripped the ball, as the text books advocate, with the first two fingers of the right hand at full stretch, so that the spin-purchase is applied by the inside of the index finger, reinforced by the *index-finger side* of the middle finger. But, whereas the instruction manuals indicate that the seam of the ball should be held alongside, and parallel to, the inside of the index finger, Laker usually held the seam at right angles to the spinning finger, I say 'usually' because, particularly on wickets responsive to spin, he often changed his grip to achieve a varying amount of turn for – so far as the batsman could observe – the same amount of spin. Without any apparent change of action he bowled a top-spinner and a ball which ran away a little off the pitch but, equally dangerously and far more unusually, he could, and did, control the *width* of his break. A number of experienced and successful spin bowlers have denied that this is possible: yet Laker achieved it by quite a number of methods – by changing the point of his grip so that his spinning finger slipped on the smooth surface of the ball instead of gripping on the seam; more fallibly, by trying to pitch the ball on the smooth surface so that it slid on; by varying the point of release; and by checking his follow-through. An elementary example of this occurred a couple of seasons ago, in a Cavaliers' match. An undergraduate batsman was facing Laker for the first time: his first ball pitched on a length and turned, quite mildly, to be met by a watchful half-cock stroke. The same thing happened to the next ball; and one almost sensed the young man deciding that this was merely another off-spinner. The third ball looked the same as the two before and the batsman moved unhurriedly across to play it, only for it to bite, turn, hurry through and hit his stumps while his bat was only half-way down.

This was characteristic of Laker's bowling. We are back with William Lillywhite's 'I s'pose if I wuz to think every ball...' In fact, Jim Laker *did* think about every ball: it was his habit to talk to himself, soundlessly, as he walked back to his mark, saying 'Now I'll give him a quicker one' or 'I'll hold this back' or 'I must make him play forward'.

Unlike some off-spinners – notably Ian Johnson and Fred Titmus – he rarely made the ball float away through the air, but his more vertical spin produced an equally puzzling dip so that although, on the whole, he tended to bowl to a full length, his overspin often caused the ball to drop shorter than the batsman expected. Above all, he spun viciously and, because he was never mechanical, he achieved his results, on turning pitches, at the lowest possible cost, while on batsmen's wickets he set problems of length and flight. His variations were subtle, designed to deceive a batsman a pitch-length away, therefore, rarely visible to spectators: but to watch a great batsman play an over of apparently identical deliveries in six different ways indicated the profundity and range of his resources.

He paid a painful physical price for his bowling. Like most men who spin the ball really hard, he often wore away the skin from the inside of his index finger. If he bowled on, it would harden, a corn would form and then, as it grew too hard, it would tear away, leaving the raw flesh exposed once more. I have sat next to him, when his side was batting, while he patiently and, as it seemed, for hours, rubbed Friar's Balsam into that tender top joint. That in itself was problem enough, but he lacked the unusually long fingers of the savage off-spinners like Goddard, Gibbs, Clay and Rowan and, to gain a similar degree of purchase, he had to take a grip which stretched his first two fingers to an exceptional and painful extent. After a few years his index finger became so distorted – the top-half of it is still bowed and thickened – that, if he rested while the raw flesh healed, an arthritic condition developed in the top finger-joint. The dual effect became chronic as he grew older: so that he frequently was unfit to play – he had, for instance, to miss the Adelaide Test of 1959 – and, even more often, he played although the pain inhibited and impaired his bowling. Ultimately it forced his retirement for, although he could still bowl well, he could no longer sustain four months of unbroken cricket.

That state of affairs was predictable, but still relatively remote, when, in 1956, as even non-cricketers can hardly help but know, he took all ten wickets of the Australians in their first innings against Surrey and, in the Test Match at Old Trafford, nine wickets of their first innings and all ten of the second. No one had ever taken all ten wickets in one innings of a Test before, and there is no other instance of nineteen in any first-class match (even the only recorded instance of eighteen occurred in a twelve-a-side game). It is, too, significant that, in each of these three performances, the bowler at the other end was Tony Lock, one of the most penetrative and competitive spin bowlers the game has ever known. Lock, we may assume, was at least partly comforted when, in the same season, he too took all ten – for Surrey against Kent – though, ironically, Laker was not playing in the match.

Jim Laker is inclined to rate his ten wickets in the Surrey v. Australians fixture as the best of the three performances. Though the wicket gave a spinner more assistance from his end than the other (Lock's), it was not outstandingly helpful, as is evidenced by the fact that the Australians scored 259 and McDonald batted for three-and-a-half hours; and that, after Laker's feat, Surrey made 347 against an Australian attack based mainly on spin. This was an outstanding piece of sustained spin bowling for, unchanged from about a quarter-past-twelve until half-past-five, he bowled 46 overs: 18 maidens: for 88 runs and ten wickets. He has always cherished having taken five of his wickets with straight balls, persuading the batsmen to play for the turn when in fact the ball went on through. In the second innings he and Lock bowled from opposite ends: Lock took seven wickets, Laker two, and Surrey became the first county for forty-four years to beat the Australians.

Laker took six wickets in the drawn first Test at Trent Bridge; three when Australia won on a 'green top' at Lord's and eleven (for 113 runs) in England's innings win at Headingley before the two sides went level to Old Trafford for the fourth game. The Australians were strongly, if not officially, critical of the dusty and rather slow pitch, which, certainly, offered no assistance to the fast bowlers who had given them their win at Lord's. On the other hand, England scored 459 against an attack in which Johnson – off-breaks – and Benaud – leg spin – bowled, between them, 94 overs for 274 runs and six wickets: and England put on 152 in 140 minutes immediately before Laker's first feat. There was no hint of the rout to come at the start of the Australian innings. Although Laker (Manchester end) and Lock (Stretford end) were brought on early, McDonald and Burke made 48 slow but sound runs before May switched round Laker and Lock. In his second over from the Stretford end – from which he took all his wickets in the match – Laker had McDonald taken in the leg trap from an off-break which seemed to dip and deceive him as to its length. Harvey came in and, before he had even begun to settle, he received an all but unplayable ball which pitched on his leg stump and, turning faster than anything else in the day, shot through his indecisive stroke and hit the top of the off. Immediately after tea, Burke edged Lock to Cowdrey at slip – the only Australian wicket that Laker did not take – and the Australian batting disintegrated in something near panic. Lock, perhaps, tried too hard and, in general, bowled too fast, though at times he turned the ball vastly.

Never was the difference between Lock – in the days of his 'old' action – and Laker more clearly demonstrated. In those days Lock took his wickets by the size and speed of his break, in which no one in the world was his superior. But, when the ball would only come through slowly, he lacked the power to defeat top-class batsmen who concentrated on defence. Laker was the constant testimony to an adage which Jack Hobbs once propounded – that good batsmen are not dismissed by swing, break or speed so often as by the mistake of playing back when they should play forward, or forward when they should play back. It was Laker's gift, by his changing curves through the air, to deceive batsmen into those errors: and it is arguable that, at Old Trafford, until the ball began to turn quickly, late on the last afternoon, he took more of his wickets by misleading the batsman as to his length than by the extent of his turn – which was the obvious but subsidiary factor of his bowling. Now he remained magnificently cool, applying his fine changes of arc and line within a close range. Miller, Archer and Benaud attempted, with no success, to hit their way out of trouble. Mackay, who had been out to Laker five times in six meetings, followed a ball which turned away from him as if hypnotized and pushed a simple catch to Oakman in the gully. In half an hour Laker bowled 22 balls for eight runs and seven wickets. His complete figures were 16.4 overs: 4 maidens: 37 runs: 9 wickets: and Australia were all out for 84.

When they followed on, McDonald and Burke again made a start steady enough to demonstrate that the pitch was deadly slow and that the ball that dismissed Harvey in the first innings was something of a freak. Again, too, Laker and Lock were brought on early but the batsmen's progress was only interrupted, with the score at 28, by McDonald retiring with cramp. Harvey took his place; his first ball from Laker was over-pitched and, moving out, he hit it off the middle of the bat, straight at Colin Cowdrey – specifically stationed at short mid-on – who made a quick, reflex-action, two-handed catch. Craig and Burke played to the end of Friday at 53 for one. After a gale during the night, there was only three quarters of an hour of play on Saturday when Australia scored six more runs and Burke, misreading Laker's flight, pushed forward too late and not far enough and the ball flicked across the bat face to Lock at short leg. McDonald resumed his innings with Craig. Monday was a day of cold, gale winds and two sessions of play adding up to an hour, during which Craig and McDonald made a careful way to 84 for two. On Tuesday, the last day, a start was made only ten minutes late on a wet pitch. May shuffled through his hand of bowlers – Statham, Bailey, Laker, Lock and Oakman – the ball turned occasionally, but only slowly, and it was Bailey who caused the few false strokes. McDonald and Craig batted until lunch at 112 for 2 wickets. For England there were four hours – and for Australia (263 behind), eight wickets – left.

Laker and Lock bowled after lunch, and at last the sun came out to dry the pitch. After a few overs May once more switched Lock and Laker to opposite ends. Again Laker took a wicket by flight as much as turn: Craig was misled into a back stroke with too little space to adjust to the turn, and was l.b.w. to an off-break he might have smothered by a forward stroke. The left-handed Mackay again haplessly followed a ball that turned away from him, and jabbed his second catch to Oakman in the gully, to complete his 'pair' in the match. Miller was drawn forward and bowled; Archer, pushing out beyond his pads, edged the off-break to short leg and, in half an hour, Laker had taken four wickets for one run. Then the sun went in, and perhaps the wicket eased; whatever the reason, Benaud settled in with McDonald. May took off Laker, for Lock and Oakman: Benaud and McDonald survived for an hour-and-a-half to tea.

Afterwards the sun shone and, without being absolutely 'sticky', the wicket, for the first and only time in the match, consistently took spin fairly quickly, Immediately Laker – now back at the Stretford end – made an off-break bite and jump at McDonald's bat and Oakman at short leg took his fifth catch of the game. McDonald had batted for over five-and-a-half hours spread from Friday to Tuesday evening – for 89. At about five o'clock Benaud went back to Laker and the off-break cut 'through the gate'. Twenty minutes more and Lindwall was taken in the leg trap: 198 for nine. Still there was no connivance to give Laker all ten wickets: this match was for The Ashes, and no one dared think of taking a risk with its outcome for the sake of a personal record. Lock was still bowling as keenly as ever: as a fact, he bowled four overs more than Laker in the innings. There was an hour left for play when Maddocks, like others before him, moved on to the back foot, again the off-break nipped through, and he was l.b.w.

England had won by an innings and 170 runs and, one-up with one to play, had retained The Ashes. Laker had performed two unique feats: he had taken all ten wickets for the second time in the season (and against the same team: the Australians, no less): and he had taken nineteen wickets in a match. While the first feat may one day be equalled, it is doubtful if the second ever will be – and surely not at Test level.

'All ten' is not simply a matter of skill; there must be a strong element of luck if no bowler takes a single wicket at the other end. In Laker's case, too, it is remarkable that the first of his ten wickets was taken on Friday evening and the last four days later, on Tuesday. At the other end, Statham, Bailey, Lock and Oakman all bowled for appreciable periods without taking a wicket. Nevertheless, this was a piece of bowling to deserve outstanding figures. He bowled on a wicket which was generally slow and, at different periods, dusty, sodden, wet, and drying. If the pitch gave him some help, it must also be remembered that he achieved his feat at the highest level of competition – against Australia, with The Ashes at issue. His figures were 51.2 overs: 23 maidens: 53 runs: 10 wickets.

The very next day, the Australians' began their second match of the tour with Surrey, a prospect that can have given them little pleasure. Rain, however, washed out the first day and reduced the third. Laker took four for 41 in the first Australian innings, and one for 17 in the truncated second. By the end of that match he had taken 103 wickets in the season – 56 of them Australian and 47 English. He harried the Australians yet again in The Oval Test, with 4 for 80 in their first innings and, after a storm, 3 for 8 in the second, before bad light ended the match. His 46 wickets (at 9.60) in the series remains a record aggregate for England v. Australia Tests and, apart from 49 by S. F. Barnes in South Africa in 1913–14, it has never been exceeded by any bowler in any Test series.

If 1956 was statistically his greatest season, he has reason to cherish his tour of Australia in 1958–59. A number of the 1953 and 1956 Australians believed that Test wickets for those series in England were specially prepared for Lock and Laker; and said openly that, if they ever faced Laker on their own good wickets, they would settle the scores of those two seasons. There is little doubt that Laker had been left out of the 1950–51 and 1954–55 teams to Australia on the old theory that 'It is no good taking an off-spinner to Australia', an argument difficult to justify since, until then, England had never within living memory picked a pure, finger-spinning, off-breaker for an Australian tour. In 1958, however, Laker was so firmly established a member of the England side that to have left him behind again would have seemed extremely odd. He made the tour and, as the Australians had foreseen, the wickets there offered little encouragement to his spin, and were signally lacking in pace. This was not merely a deep probing of his technique but a contest in which, on the Australian side at least, there was a degree of 'needle' amounting in some instances to bitterness. He came out of it with infinite credit. England never won a single Test, and Laker was handicapped throughout by the arthritic finger condition which prevented him from playing in the Adelaide Test. But he bowled more overs than any other English bowler in the series, and took more wickets – 15 of the 45 Australian wickets that fell in the Tests when he played – and finished first in the Test averages. If the Australians grudged, or at least qualified, credit for his bowling in 1956, they could not withold it when, with the conditions completely against him, and against opponents who were in a dominating position, he bowled with such control, accuracy, flight and artifice that he was never collared.

This should have been a high note on which to close his Test career: but he did not do so happily. At the end of the 1959 season he retired from the Surrey staff and, in the following year, published a book describing his last few seasons in first-class cricket and stating clearly what he felt to be justified grievances. In punishment he was beaten with the official stick which had been prepared for cricketers who wrote – or lent their names to – books of a deliberately sensational character. Laker's book, I am convinced, was not intended to be sensational but only to state a case in which he felt entitled to a hearing. Some of its contents, however, were given sensational press-treatment and, as a result, Laker's honorary membership of M.C.C. – probably the greatest honour that can be paid to a cricketer – was withdrawn. Happily, he was reinstated in 1967.

Meanwhile, after two seasons out of the first-class game, he was persuaded to turn out in occasional matches for Essex. The state of his spinning-finger did not allow him to play regularly, but he had much experience of value to impart to the younger players and, in 12 matches of 1962 and 10 of 1963, he bowled effectively enough to finish top of the county's bowling averages. By then he had ceased to regard his batting seriously, but a correct player, at his most competent against pace, he had made two centuries for Surrey and played at least three extremely valuable innings in Test cricket. He was, too, in his early days, a capable field in the gully, where he made some rapid stops and catches.

As a man he has always been, in manner as in his cricket, clear-sighted and thoughtful; he is positive in his principles, firm in his loyalties and has a dry and, sometimes sardonic, sense of humour: the mind's eye recalls him walking away at the end of an over, head tilted back and, from under a high-pointing cap-peak, looking up into the sky and grinning widely at some private joke. He has planned his career carefully and devotes himself conscientiously to his business affairs. He married his Austrian wife, Lilly, in 1951, and they and their two daughters make a friendly household in Putney.

Jim Laker has been more clear-sighted than some members of his profession in accepting that a cricketer's playing career must come to an end, and that the wise man does not linger too long on the stage. If his fingers sometimes itch to bowl – as they do – he is wise enough not to recriminate; and, in any case, he can console himself with the knowledge that for some years he was – and deeply enjoyed being – the undisputed master of his own department of the game of cricket.

EIGHT

Trueman and Statham
by Frank Tyson

1

IN SUCH AN openly extrovert pursuit as fast bowling, humility is an unlooked-for characteristic. Rather does one expect a certain arrogance: the brimming confidence that no bowler in this world can be more frighteningly effective – the vociferous assurance that no batsman can withstand his fury. This perhaps was the magnificent self-conceit which led Kortright, the Essex fast bowler, to explode to a questioner, 'Swing? No, sir, I just bowl fast and dare them to cut me!' Yet there are times when even we egocentrics, finding ourselves in the presence of, or being compared to some contemporaneous colossus, experience a complete feeling of inadequacy. What a sense of inferiority lies in equation to Lindwall, Miller, Davidson, Hall – or closer to home, Trueman and Statham!

Description of such bowlers beggars the ordinary terminology of cricket; one begins to bandy about the word – 'great'. But what exactly do we mean to convey by this frequently used, more often prostituted word? Do we apply it to those players endowed with a high degree of natural ability? – the great swingers of the ball like Lindwall or Bart King? – the out-and-out pace men such as Hall and Griffith? – the exponents of variation, subtle in pace and length – the Spofforths and the Barnes of this cricketing world? Can it be that the bowling elite are the men who produced the performance for the occasion – the Test temperament men?

Comparisons are necessarily invidious things, clouded and coloured as they are by time and prejudice. Those Australian cricket followers of the '20's and '30's who witnessed the ascendancy of McDonald, Gregory and Larwood, find it hard to comprehend that they could be surpassed in the peculiar skills. Even figures, therefore, are meaningful only when averages are set above the quotients of time, pitches and circumstance. Seventy-five Test wickets garnered over eight years in selective corners of the cricketing world is clearly not as significantly a 'great' record as three hundred and seven collected from every cranny of international cricket, as a member of both successful and unsuccessful teams. For me at least, the title of 'great' goes only to those whose careers embrace a temporal and geographical breadth, and the universality of whose experience is reflected commensurately in their Test analyses.

With 307 Test victims to his credit, and a first-class career which has spanned some seventeen years and the world four times, Freddie must be deemed to have fulfilled all the necessary criteria. His international record stands second to no fast bowler in the world. His wanderings on behalf of cricket have taken him repeatedly to Australia, the West Indies and New Zealand, and would have taken him further afield had it not been for his own ebullient and fractious non-selective character. Like some craggy obelisk adorning the market-place of his own Northern towns, he has been at the heart of every Yorkshire Eleven since 1949, as if commemorating the passing of less-lasting souls. The Coxons, the Foords, the Whiteheads and the Cowans have been and gone but Trueman, like the Yorkshire Ouse, goes on, apparently for ever.

Physically he hardly seemed destined for athletic greatness. Indeed his sporting prowess was limited to the soccer and cricket fields and an amazing adeptness on the more restrictive, yet nonetheless demanding billiard table. He was no Greek statue, but the truncated breadth of his characteristically square fast-bowler's frame was lined with an even strength from shoulder to hip. His feet, those ploughmen of many a batsman's wicket, like those of most great athletes, turned in and imparted their bent to his pillared legs. Even the square lines of his jaw – always prematurely dark-bearded around five o'clock – bespoke a certain pugnacity and power. He was puissant in back and long in arm, just like all of the mining fast bowlers who over the years, Yorkshire, Derbyshire and Nottinghamshire have all whistled up to the surface. His upbringing never deserted him and even in the torrid sun and climate of Australia and the West Indies he retained his inborn underground fear of sunburn. On Bondi Beach, amongst so much bronzed flesh, his pallor made me realise why Australians call Englishmen, 'Pommies'.

But there was nothing incongruous about Trueman's bowling. His parabolic approach from the regions of a straightish mid-off was rhymically smooth, and stridingly long. Only the portly advance of years curtailed the long circular swing of his classically erect left guiding arm. At the bowling wicket his action was faultless in its body-swing, his bared, sparsely-haired chest effronting the sensibilities of mid-on and his metalled right toe braking the

FRED TRUEMAN 'Outwardly at least, he assumed the mantle of greatness with complete self-assurance. He was the Cassius Clay of fast bowling'

BRIAN STATHAM 'Statham's accuracy was legend in contemporary cricket, and as much respected by batsmen as he himself was looked up to as one of the country's senior professionals'

pent-up power of his troublesome final seven-league stride until the last volcanic moment. His follow-through was the batsman's nightmare and the umpire's bane, churning up large arable areas outside the suffering left-hander's off-stump. But such was Trueman's control of the mere mechanics of bowling that he seldom permitted such trivialities as a no-ball or a request to run off the pitch to disturb his confidence. He merely adjusted his drag or ran wider on the crease. His delivery, like that of his hearty fellow-tradesman Lindwall, was perfectly suited to out-swing, a ball on which most of his effectiveness was based. By comparison to his boomeranging outcurve, his inswinger was a puny thing – at least to everyone except Fred. Even the Australian wickets, enervating on man and ball alike, could not curb his movement to the slips.

His very first ball in Australia, in 1958, resulted in West Australian batsman Jack Rutherford being caught in the slips: a moving performance which had the succeeding batsmen probing for another five overs. In 1963, his magnificent use of the second new ball in the second inning of the Melbourne Test and his subsequent five wickets tipped the balance in England's favour; I can still remember his dismissals of Benaud and O'Neill – the flashing bat, the edge, and the surprising agility of Cowdrey at first slip. There was an amazing resilience in his bouncer – enough to send it steepling over the head of many batsmen. To the ambitious hooker it always presented a challenge – sometimes successfully met, at others, painfully suffered. Even when he bowled a standard length, Trueman elicited disproportionate bounce from the pitch; it was just as if he hit the wicket as hard as he would have liked to strike the batsman.

Outwardly at least, he assumed the mantle of greatness with complete self-assurance. He was the Cassius Clay of fast bowling and whilst he did not always state that he was the greatest, one always felt that his mastery was founded on this confidence. Other bowlers toiled when the air was swingless, the ball without shine and the wicket barren of response. But Fred knew, as if with the certainty of faith, that he was still moving, cutting off the pitch, deviating off the seam – even if the wicketkeeper himself was not aware of it. It was a graphic experience, to listen to his description of a straight ball, missed by some wretched batsman – how it swung late to the slips and came back off the wicket. It was a brand of confidence based on the knowledge that in fact he could perform these feats when conditions suited him. Allied to it was a fierce pugnacity towards all batsmen, but more particularly towards those who were unwise enough to bat in that harlequinade headgear which Fred loathingly termed a 'jazz-hat'. Cambridge and Oxford batsmen have been known to lose all heart for the game after having met Fred on these colourful terms. Only rarely did his mask of confidence and hate slip – when as at Sydney in 1958 the wicket was hopeless in pace. But even then it was but a momentary lapse. It only needed the encouragement of a wicket to bring him roaring back.

I suppose that deep down Trueman was motivated by that unreasoning, mad-cap, fast bowling force – the earnest desire to bowl really quick. In his declining years he still considered himself just as fast as on the day in Hull in 1949 when I saw him for the first time. Then he was a raw eighteen; at the moment of delivery his head was flung back and his gaze intent upon loftier things than the stumps. Nonetheless the Army batsmen, Geoffrey Keighley, the Yorkshire captain, and his fellow-fieldsmen will tell you that he was even at that early stage, very fast. This was a painful testimony which was to be vouchsafed by the unfortunate Indian batsmen when they met him for the first time in tests some three short years later. In that particular rubber he collected no fewer than twenty-nine wickets.

I often wonder whether that first Test of Trueman's in 1952 was all the more important because he was representing his country or because he was performing before his very own Headingley crowd. Certainly there stood behind his whole cricketing career the ultimate pride in his status as an international player; but the very prop of his cricketing existence was his unswerving allegiance to Yorkshire and his joy in all things emanating from the County of the Broad Acres. All over the world he met expatriate Yorkshiremen and rejoiced in their company. When in 1953 he became the first Yorkshireman to win the Cricket Writer's award for the Best Young Cricketer of the Year, his first avowed public intent was to take the trophy back to Yorkshire, where in the northern air, its lustre would undoubtedly be the greater. The reference was apposite since I have often felt that no Bradford fog could ever dim the significance of a cricket honour in a Yorkshireman's eyes. Cricket to the Headingley habitué is just as much a cause for pride as York Minister. He knows full well that his side 'laikes' better than any of the other sixteen counties – any other sixteen countries for that matter!

This external enthusiasm finds reflection in a feeling of reciprocal inter-dependence within the playing camp. Naturally enough over the years, the team has incorporated personalities of widely differing and, at times, dissident temperaments; yet rarely does this lack of unanimity intrude on the field. For his part, Trueman has been constantly blessed throughout the course of seventeen summers with wholehearted catching support close to the wicket: such grasping presences as Wilson, Close, Halliday, Lowson and Sharpe. When he encountered snags of bowling technique there were the tutelage and shoulders of Bill Bowes and Freddie's kindred spirit, Alec Coxon on which to lean. Matters of general guidance came more within the ken of Brian Sellars.

It has been suggested that Trueman's successes over the years would have been the greater had his undoubted physical ability been harnessed to a more penetrating intelligence. In my eyes, such observations themselves lack observation. There dwelt within Trueman an innate bowling shrewdness – his ready wit gave ample evidence of a lively brain at work. He seemed to know where to bowl as if by instinct; moreover he remembered batsmen's foibles and weaknesses. I scarcely remember the time when he did not completely demoralise his favourite Nottinghamshire and Somerset batsmen. In the third Test against Australia in 1961 he was acute enough to analyse the cutting propensities of the Leeds wicket, shorten his run and end the match with an analysis of 11 for 88. Off the field, there was a note of cynical wit behind his every remark; his anecdotes which, though more often than not unsuitable for the drawing-room, were pointedly pertinent and genuinely funny.

As a batsman Trueman was imbued with the same refractory pugnacity as found expression in his bowling. I can still see him today, striding his crushing way out to the Adelaide wicket in the fourth Test of 1959, his cap pulled down in slanting aggression and his bat grasped in his wringing right hand like some unfortunate opponent. How vociferously he expressed his disappointment at 'bagging a pair' in our ten wicket defeat! Fred undoubtedly valued his wicket as I once found out when I ran him out. It was only a festival match, but the denizens of the Scarborough pavilion probably still retain the audible image of his return from the crease. I know my mother told me later that she never imagined that cricketers said such things! Once, when I was panting on the threshold of my hundred wickets for the season, Fred held me firmly at bay for a full half-hour and eventually denied me the honour. For him there was no easy way to any bowling milestone. I think he batted all the better for his appreciation of the difficulties of bowling; his attitude was 'I have to bowl them out, they can b—y well bowl me out!'

Nor was his batting ambition just false pride, as the century-suffering bowlers of Northants, Middlesex and Young England can testify. True, his technique was not the balletomane's delight, based firmly as it was on a weighty forward prod, a flailing back-foot drive into the covers, and an assortment of passably correct herculean heaves both straight and on the leg-side. Though they were aesthetically lacking, his methods often proved crashingly and dangerously effective. In the fashion direct they frequently rescued his team from total inadequacy.

More than any other one aspect of his batting skill, Fred was inordinately proud of his long hitting. At Park Lane, Bradford, I have seen him repeatedly hoist Northants slow left-hand bowler, Vince Broderick, over the lofty football stand some hundred yards distant – and scowl to himself when he fell short. In his own mind there were no limits to the distance he could dispatch the ball. During a Champion County versus the Rest game at the Oval, Barrington caught Trueman – a hundred yard on-drive which he despairingly grasped as he teetered on the nethermost edge of the Vauxhall boundary. 'It would have gone for six,' explained Fred in the dressing-room later, 'if I hadn't hit it with the top edge'.

His acrobatic versatility at short-leg afforded a hint as to where his batting ability originated; his reflexes were as quick as his own repartee and his reactions were proportionately tuned. At short-leg, his chosen station, he was a formidable proposition, breathing hostility down the very shirt-neck of the batsman and engulfing catches like some great long-tongued chameleon fastening on to flies. Those who saw the on-side trio of Lock, Oakman, and Trueman in the Australian Test at Manchester in 1956 will not readily forget them, squatting like out-of-work miners on their haunches, waiting eagerly to put the finishing touches to Laker's wizardry. That day the Aussies were not misled by Trueman's cheerful banter between the overs; he was often like that – outwardly light-hearted, but within, deadly serious.

De Buffon observed, *'Le style est l'homme même'*. Of Trueman he would probably have said, *'L'homme est le style même'*. For the man was as forthright as his bowling. There were no barriers of affectation between himself and his audience, whether his listeners were West Indian administrators, London 'society' or the cargo-ship's crew whom he once invited up to his Brisbane hotel room. Because he treated all and sundry to the genuine Trueman, he made legions of friends in all walks of life.

One minute in the Melbourne Test of 1958 he was ceremoniously doffing his cap in acknowledgement of the Southern stand's acclamation of some ostentatious piece of fielding; the next, he was giving them a visible demonstration of what he thought of their vocal opinion of his bowling. There was no mistaking his flair for such showmanship. Having returned the ball to the keeper with his right hand, he would, on occasions demonstrate his ability to do the same with his left. In social games he has been known to bowl both left and right-handed. Such flamboyance inevitably brought the house down – and Freddie thrived on encouragement. To laugh at one of his anecdotes was to bring forth a wealth of stories which I still find difficult to imagine inside the head of one man. Moreover, as a raconteur he was sans pareil, possessing an acute sense of the humorous, a pithy Yorkshire delivery and a vocabulary which though often blasphemously punctuated, was tolerated equally well in Government House as it was in the Public Bar.

The truth was that he was no snob – nor yet an inverted snob. His human unsophisticated qualities brought him invitations to the billiard table of Sir Robert George, Governor of South Australia, and to snooker games in Working Men's Clubs. The high regard of Australia's former Prime Minister, Sir Robert Menzies, for the Yorkshire bowler was amply demonstrated in Canberra in 1963, when on the eve of the Prime Minister's match he presented Fred with an inscribed beer tankard. It was perhaps, the only time I have ever seen the England bowler moved by an emotion which was not spleen. 'To think,' he said, 'even the b—y Prime Minister of Australia remembers my birthday!'

His individuality and non-conformism made him an unstable element in the composition of any touring party. He was never amenable to discipline nor gregariously submissive in his attitude, as quickly became clear to me in 1958 when I witnessed a few 'conversations' between Trueman and that other equally obdurate personality, M.C.C. manager, Freddie Brown. Charlie Palmer, player-manager of the 1953–54 tour to the West Indies must have also experienced some of these forceful talks. It was probably some of Trueman's lack of conventionality during these latter conversations and the West Indian tour which led to his omission from the 1954–55 side to Australia, my inclusion, and my subsequent season of success. Not that there was any degree of personal rivalry between us, I liked him. Indeed I had the unique – or in deference to his wife I should say – almost unique experience of accompanying him on his honeymoon. It was a coach trip – a sponsored coach trip – to Nice. A journey never to be forgotten: an incident-packed fortnight including diatribes on the inopportune and undesirable somnolent qualities of red-wine, the public dubbing of the hotel's very gallic Maître d'Hotel as 'chuff', and the regaling of his fellow-passengers with a broadcast stream of songs and stories which continued throughout the length of France.

This then is Freddie Trueman, as I saw him: a Yorkshireman and a fast-bowler – to his mind the finest of all possible combinations. It may well prove that someone will eventually surpass his three hundred and seven Test wickets, though as Fred said: 'He will be b—y tired.' It is possible that someone will usurp his mathematical claim to being England's greatest fast bowler. Yet people will always remember Trueman as truly great; and the adjective will not merely describe his cricketing ability.

2

Life shows us that an outwardly incompatible couple often make the best partners. It is hard to see any other reason why over the years the histrionic Freddie and the undemonstrative Brian Statham constituted one of the most feared fast-bowling duets in international cricket. Statham was the very antithesis of almost everything Trueman embodied – save the one important factor of effectiveness.

Unlike the Yorkshireman, Statham gave the lie-direct to the

generalisation that fast bowlers are extroverts. He was as emotionally self-contained as Trueman was out-giving. When he bowled the first ball of the Adelaide Test in 1959, the delivery pitched six inches outside Colin McDonald's off-stump and snapped back to pass a half-millimetre over the top of middle. McDonald subsequently went on to score 170; but save for his instinctive clutch at his forehead, Statham never displayed any emotion – nor indeed did he mention again that first back-breaking, heart-breaking delivery.

Behind Statham's bowling there was a fundamental, humane commonsense, as was admirably borne out by an incident during one of the Lancashire bowler's visits to the West Indies. Whilst the ethics of cricket's fast-bowling fraternity are not set out in black and white, it is considered unfitting to ply fellow, non-batting bowlers with bouncers. But the West Indian giant who hit Jim Laker over the eye must not have been a member of the bowler's union. He gashed Laker's forehead so badly that it took a five minute pursuit all over the field and a ten minute talk to persuade Jim that he had not lost an eye. When subsequently, the West Indian bowler reluctantly took his guard at the batting crease, Trueman was in favour of physical retaliation. 'Nay,' said Statham, 'I think I'll just bowl him out!'

If there was ever a quiet man of touring cricket Statham was he. Not that he did not mix. He did – he was one of the boys. But not for him the cigars and the champagne – 'the soda pop' – of the social side of the trip. His preferred drink was an ale in the bar, his favourite smoke, the perpetual cigarette which never seemed to leave his mouth, and his usual breakfast, 'a cough and a cup of coffee'.

But all was not quiescent in Statham's cricket. There was within a dislike of batsmen which though it did not burn brightly was nonetheless frightening in its smouldering intensity. Sometimes it found its expression in a most alarming bouncer: a boring, hypnotic, throttling ball which seemed to follow the batsman in his retreat.

Moreover there was about Statham an aura of stubbornness; a trait which came out not only in his bowling but in such small matters as his name. He would insist on being called 'George'. Why? Simply because he liked it.

His heart, that essential of fast bowlers, was of sufficient strength to carry him through not only fifteen years of Test cricket, but also through almost two decades of Lancashire cricket. During the recent lean times of Lancastrian failure, a bevy of successive captains have known only one remedy for any shortcomings in their attack: 'Bring on Statham.' It was a call which he never shirked, even when he, as captain, had the power to decide when the flesh felt weak.

But greatness – and Statham certainly had it – does not lie merely in dedication and perseverance. 'George' had many other facets to his character and to his art. He was, for instance, completely 'unflappable' in temperament and in cricketing terms this was translated into a combination of length and direction which was virtually an immaculate concept. Many opinions, indeed, stated paradoxically that Statham's control was too perfect. Every county batsman between 1950 and 1966 knew with the certainty born of experience that ninety-per-cent of Statham's deliveries would pitch on a length and in line with the stumps. Thus the game was reduced to a contest of mathematical exactitude and the element of physical fear, often a telling weapon in the fast bowler's armoury, was drastically reduced. Brian had a name for this favourite delivery of his: he called it his 'dead-on ball'. Indeed there could be little which was more straight than his bowling philosophy. 'If you bowl every ball on the off-side,' he would say, 'you need all your fieldsmen on the off. If you bowl every ball on the leg-side, then you need all your men on that side of the wicket. But if you bowl straight – then all you need is a wicketkeeper' – this was spoken with a gleam in his eye.

Statham's accuracy was a legend in contemporary cricket, and as much respected by batsmen as he himself was looked up to as one of the country's senior professionals. Once during a country game in South Africa, when, unnoticed by the captain I had surreptitiously insinuated myself into the slips, I was surprised, after six balls had been sent down by 'George', to hear Godfrey Evans comment on Brian's lack of form on that particular day. His conclusion was based on the fact that Statham in his first over, had actually sent down two deliveries which did not pitch in line with the stumps – definitely a sub-Statham performance.

This 'nasty, nagging length' as he himself used to call it, made Statham the perfect foil for bowlers less accurate than himself. To escape from Statham was for a batsman to experience a feeling of sublime release; to feel that 'now at last I can play a few shots and score a few runs'. A relaxation in vigilance, a lapse in concentration, and the bowler at the other end to Statham reaped the reward of someone else's persistent effort.

This in a nutshell told the story of the 1954–55 M.C.C. tour of Australia. The glamour of success was undoubtedly mine. When in the second innings of the Sydney Test, I captured 6 for 45, few spared a thought for Statham who on that day bowled unremittingly for two hours into a stiff breeze and took 3 for 45. In the third Test at Melbourne, on an increasingly variable wicket, he accounted for five Australian wickets for sixty, at a time in the second innings of the game when the pitch was probably at its best. Yet in the public eye these figures declined into unimportance by the side of my last innings return of 7 for 27; an analysis which incorporated two deflections on to the stumps and two near miraculous catches and which certainly owed much to the desperation injected into the batsmen's methods by Statham's relentless pursuit. To me it felt like having Menuhin playing second fiddle to my lead.

'George' only swung the ball rarely and when he did the complexity of angles often baffled him. He was a straightforward craftsman. Once in British Guiana, where the cricket ground, constructed on reclaimed land, lay below sea level, the humidity was such that even Statham swung, disconcertingly and uncontrollably. I cannot but wonder whether in fact he ever bowled a wide; if he did, that was the occasion it could have happened.

One must not pre-suppose that his straight-from-the-shoulder approach incorporated no subtleties whatsoever. His *'specialité de la maison'* was the 'nip-backer', as he called it; a ball which, in the days before the refinement of swerve and swing became the rage, was apparently the stock-in-trade of every fast bowler. Its line was generally somewhere in the region of six inches outside the off-stump and its break-back brought it quickly back into the middle. Woe betide the batsman who did not play close to his pads, for Statham was the most accurate discoverer of 'garden gates' in the whole game of cricket.

Personally I was always more than a little sceptical about 'George's' ability to bowl the 'nip-backer' whenever he wished. At least, that was the case before I met John Gunn. The old man sat on my right hand at a Master's luncheon – a periodic meal held in a Fleet Street restaurant to honour the late 'Master' Sir Jack Hobbs. Chubby Tate sat on my left. Politeness and ignorance demanded that I should inquire of John Gunn his special place in the Nottinghamshire cricket scene which I knew he frequented at the turn of the century. Imagine my scepticism therefore when he told me that in addition to batting, he also bowled breaks – at about my pace! Furthermore he maintained that he could do this at will! My doubt turned to near-credulity, however, when seizing an orange from the nearby dessert bowl and scoring a seam on it with a fruit knife, he proceeded to demonstrate how he brought the ball back off the wicket.

The reason behind my conversion was that I was looking at precisely the same fruitful grip that Brian Statham had shown me some months earlier; the hold which procured his 'nip-backer' – an outswing grip with both fore and second finger on the left-hand side of the seam. This particular delivery made Statham a deadly proposition on wickets which held even the slightest promise of movement, since even when his back-break failed to function, there was more than a possibility that the ball would carry on towards the slips off the most upright of seams. The slope of the lively old Lords wicket, and freshets of rain once brought him one of his more rewarding days – 7 for 39 in England's seventy-one run victory over South Africa in 1955. He always performed well on the hospitable surface of Lords – as the Australians discovered in 1961 when, against Statham and Trueman, they lost five wickets in scoring the seventy-one runs they needed to defeat England.

In pace Statham was deceptive. The very smoothness of his action belied the whip of his over-extended right elbow and this in turn skidded the ball on to the jarring bat of the surprised batsman. There was no Trueman-like pounding of the ball into the wicket. Indeed, if I did not fear the scorn of the physicists, I should say that the factor of the pitch mattered little to Statham's pace; if anything, he appeared to make haste off the wicket. It is not generally recognised nor acknowledged that the Lancashireman was one of England's fastest bowlers. Yet in Wellington, New Zealand, when he and I were measured electronically to gauge our respective speeds, he was a bare one mile per hour outside my figure of eighty-nine miles per hour; and, it must be added, these returns came from a saturated wicket and approaches, with

Statham not even bothering to remove his sweater nor change into his cricketing trousers! As if all these attributes were not enough, George was possessed of a yorker which, outside Lindwall and perhaps Griffith, has never been emulated in accuracy. As if drawn by a magnet, it inevitably pitched on the batsman's toes. If the striker were lucky he was bowled; but the less fortunate usually went down as if their legs had been amputated at the knees. All these skills were allied to a heart which was larger, if anything than those of the Sydney costermonger's lettuces – and they had hearts as big as Freddie Brown's. Only once have I seen Statham really dejected, when, after bowling his heart out in the second Test in Melbourne in 1959 and returning figures of 7 for 57, England collapsed against Meckiff and, dismissed for 87 in their second innings, found themselves bowling a second time after only a three or four hour's respite. Statham's action meant that on the unyielding Australian wickets his left-foot jarred at every ball against the toe of his boot, which anchored unmovingly in the firm surface. This repeated operation eventually bruised and finally removed the big toe nail, and after some three weeks of bowling over the testing holiday time of Christmas, his left big toe was quite literally – a bloody mess. Yet in the Melbourne Test of 1955 he bowled for two complete Australian innings afflicted by this most painful and unavoidable injury. It was probably the only time in a test match when a bowler has sent down some forty overs with the toe-cap of his left boot cut away and his big toe protruding.

Physically and in technique, Statham could not have differed more from his partner Trueman. The Yorkshireman's smoothness of action had a rugged strength whereas Statham's amounted almost to a fluidity; a quality which owed much to the fact that he was double jointed in the shoulders. Perhaps now, those spectators who have seen Statham divest himself of his sweater by the simple – or not so simple – expedient of grasping its hem over the top of his left shoulder will understand how he was able to do it. *'Suaviter in modo'* could be applied to every facet of his bowling. There was a limp relaxation in his approach; an attribute which brought down upon his head the additional soubriquets of 'Greyhound' and 'the Whippet'. His right foot, the very pedestal of his delivery stride, sometimes grounded on the spikeless edge of his boot. On such occasions it was not unusual to see him slip and crumple on the flinty Australian bowling creases. Yet I have never seen him injure himself in this way. It was almost as if he were boneless and as immune from fractured hurts as a jellyfish.

The self-same suavity was evident in his fielding. Many have been the batsmen who have discovered too late that, in taking their second run to deep third man, they have grossly underestimated Statham's effortless overtaking of the ball and his explosive arm.

Would that I could extend the same glowing description to George's left-handed brand of batting – an art, which, perhaps because he appreciated more keenly than most all of its fallibilities, he treated in somewhat jocular vein. He summed up his own capabilities as residing in two principal shots: the straight-batted block and the cross-batted slog. Yet even these severely-strictured batting gifts occasionally proved invaluable. In 1954 in Sydney he and Appleyard added 46 for England's very last wicket; and after all England only scraped home by 38! At Adelaide in 1959 his unbeaten 36 raised England from the very mediocre 9 for 188 to a finally more respectable 240 all out. It did not avoid the ten wickets defeat, but without his runs that loss would have been by the margin of an innings. No one was less expectant of runs than George. Yet he registered the occasional half-century in each county season, and when he did, there was scarcely a player in the county Championship who begrudged him his obvious enjoyment.

This then was 'George' Statham, a comfortable companionable cricketer; the tourist *'par excellence'*. Throughout his international and county career his task never fell below the level of the arduous. Yet he fulfilled his obligations with a philosophic dedication and a zest for the game itself. He was an out-and-out family man whose home life was interrupted only by England's mandatory demands abroad. One could scarcely say that he was blessed with good fortune. Never has there lived a bowler who so consistently shaved bat and stumps without statistical result. Even his tours were marred by family illnesses or car accidents. He allowed himself few luxuries save that of his infrequent fallow winter with his feet up, just watching the 'telly', or the less infrequent glass of beer. For me he is epitomised by that picture which I shall always carry of him in my mind – propped up against my father-in-law's fridge, that source of cold solace, after a gruelling if successful day in the second Test at Melbourne in 1955. 'Gee,' he said in his own portmanteau idiom, 'you bowled like a ding-bat.' But then so had he, he always did.

Even though my nine-year-old son's ambitions lie at the moment in the direction of batsmanship, this will not prevent him from asking, when he reaches the age of cricketing appreciation and realises that Trueman and Statham were my contemporaries, how great they were compared to other bowlers and to one another. The query is as inevitable as the old chestnuts which invariably crop up at smoke-nights or sporting panels: who was the best batsman you bowled against? – or – was Lindwall a better bowler than Miller?

For me, the question of comparison with other bowlers holds no fear of equivocation. My answer is conditioned by the fact that Statham and Trueman came to bowlerhood at a time, when though the dross age of their art in the post-war period had not yet received the alchemists golden touch, the precious transformation had begun. Subsequently they deposed the declining giant Bedser, and led the van at the very apogee of England's fast bowling renaissance, outvying such men as Moss, Loader, Jackson, Flavell and Rhodes and enduring to outpace the new breed of Larter and Snow. At a time when every first-class county accounted themselves poor without a genuine fast bowler, Lancashire and Yorkshire were doubly blessed in the persons of Statham and Trueman.

On the subject of the comparative assessment of the two bowlers I find myself, understandably I feel, biassed by virtue of my successful association with the Lancashire man. The spirit of impartiality, however, moves me to a mathematical analysis of their respective merits. Bearing in mind Mark Twain's opinion that there are three kinds of factual statements, statistics, damned statistics and lies, I shall confine myself to the general conclusion rather than the particular example. The career records of Statham and Trueman reveal that Fred has enjoyed just one more first-class season than Brian. Yet during his briefer span, Statham has played in more Tests: an item which is counterbalanced by the fact that though the Yorkshireman has represented his country on fewer occasions, he has, in his more limited opportunities, captured more wickets. In the sphere of county cricket the Lancashire bowler has reaped fewer victims yet at a much cheaper cost. Strangely enough, he has been more consistent than Trueman, bowling his way to the seasonal hundred wickets mark thirteen times compared to the Yorkshireman's twelve. To avoid the accusation of partisanship, I must admit that Trueman's lack of Statham's factual consistency was due in no small way, to an interregnum of two years in the R.A.F. One must admit, however, that Trueman's international opportunities, particularly overseas, would have been the greater, had it not been for his own stormy-petrel disposition. His touring trips numbered only four, whereas Statham was England's number one fast-bowling choice for every M.C.C. side overseas between the years 1954–62: his foreign excursions amounted to no fewer than eight. My own subjective assessment of the respective merits of the two bowlers leave me in no doubt that Trueman in his day and age was the most effective fast striking force England has seen. He was the master of shock tactics, the bane of tail-end batsmen and four times the taker of the coveted first-class hat-trick; like Wes Hall he was a fearsome opponent regarded in awe by all batsmen alike.

Statham was more the counterpart of Hambledon's honest yeomen; a loyal and untiring servant of his club and country. He never refused a tour for which he was needed; he visited India – a country for which most fast bowlers' enthusiasm waxes faintly and wanes quickly – and in Australia he toiled at times when his sole means of support was the ineffective Warr and the medium-pace of Freddie Brown. Why, only in 1967 he laboured long for Lancashire, taking his usual hundred wickets and finishing third in the national averages.

I am proud to say that I once bowled at the other end to Freddie Trueman – Mr Wilson did not exaggerate when he designated him a great Yorkshireman. But I cannot rid myself of the opinion that true greatness transcends supreme competency in a chosen field of activity; I cannot but feel that it must incorporate a more rounded human accomplishment. I perhaps expressed this sentiment indirectly to a Melbourne Twenty Nine Club dinner held in honour of Brian Statham. 'Many people are proud to acknowledge acquaintance with a famous fast bowler and say – Fred Trueman was a friend of mine. But of Statham, most people who have met him are even prouder to say – I knew Brian; he was my mate.'

NINE

Statistics
by Michael Fordham

SYDNEY FRANCIS BARNES
b 19.4.1873   d 26.12.1967

Warwickshire, Lancashire, Staffordshire and England

CAREER IN FIRST-CLASS CRICKET

	RUNS	WKTS.	AVGE.	5 WKTS. INNINGS	10 WKTS. MATCH
1895	145	3	48.33	–	–
1896	54	0	–	–	–
1899	161	4	40.25	–	–
1901	99	6	16.50	1	–
1901–02 (Aust.)	676	41	16.48	5	2
1902	2,049	95	21.56	7	1
1903	2,339	131	17.85	12	3
1907	68	2	34.00	–	–
1907–08 (Aust.)	1,185	54	21.94	5	1
1909	537	34	15.79	3	–
1911	350	14	25.00	1	–
1911–12 (Aust.)	1,231	59	20.86	4	–
1912	782	69	11.33	8	3
1913	351	35	10.02	4	1
1913–14 (S. Af.)	1,117	104	10.74	13	5
1914	144	8	18.00	–	–
1927	191	7	27.28	–	–
1928	205	20	10.25	3	1
1929	465	29	16.03	2	1
1930	140	4	35.00	–	–
	12,289	719	17.09	68	18

CAREER IN TEST CRICKET

MATCHES	BALLS	MDNS.	RUNS	WKTS.	AVGE.	5 WKTS. INNINGS	10 WKTS. MATCH
27	7,873	358	3,106	189	16.43	24	7

DEBUT MATCH: Warwickshire v. Derbyshire (Birmingham) 1895.
BEST BOWLING: Nine wickets in innings (1).
            9-103 England v. South Africa (Johannesburg) 1913–14.
N.B. Barnes took 8-56 in the first innings of this match for a match analysis of 17-159.
'HAT-TRICKS' (1): England v. The Rest (Oval) 1912.

MAURICE WILLIAM TATE
b 29.4.1895 d 18.5.1956
Sussex and England
CAREER IN FIRST-CLASS CRICKET

	RUNS	WKTS.	AVGE.	5 WKTS. INNINGS	10 WKTS. MATCH
1912	28	1	28.00	–	–
1913	193	11	17.54	–	–
1914	352	10	35.20	–	–
1919	1,339	48	27.89	–	–
1920	1,466	71	20.64	2	1
1921	1,774	70	25.34	2	–
1922	2,073	119	17.42	7	–
1923	3,061	219	13.97	17	6
1924	2,818	205	13.74	17	4
1924–25 (Aust.)	1,464	77	19.01	7	2
1925	3,415	228	14.97	24	10
1926	2,575	147	17.51	12	4
1926–27 (India)	1,599	116	13.78	10	2
1927	3,018	147	20.53	10	2
1928	3,184	165	19.29	14	3
1928–29 (Aust.)	1,325	44	29.88	1	–
1929	2,903	156	18.60	11	4
1930	2,449	123	19.91	10	1
1930–31 (S. Af.)	621	33	18.81	3	–
1931	2,179	141	15.45	8	2
1932	2,494	160	15.58	11	1
1932–33 (Aust. and N.Z.)	356	14	25.42	–	–
1933	1,808	99	18.26	7	–
1934	2,796	142	19.69	9	2
1935	2,141	113	18.94	6	–
1936	1,748	78	22.41	7	–
1937	1,365	46	29.67	–	–
	50,544	2,783	18.16	195	44

CAREER IN TEST CRICKET

						5 WKTS.	10 WKTS.
MATCHES	BALLS	MDNS.	RUNS	WKTS.	AVGE.	INNINGS	MATCH
39	12,571	579	4,051	155	26.13	7	1

DEBUT MATCH: Sussex v. Northamptonshire (Northampton) 1912.
BEST BOWLING: Nine wickets in innings (1).
9-71 Sussex v. Middlesex (Lord's) 1926.
BEST BOWLING IN TEST CRICKET: 6-42 England v. South Africa (Leeds) 1924.
'HAT-TRICKS' (3): Sussex v. Middlesex (Lord's) 1926.
Rest of England v. Lancashire (Oval) 1926.
Sussex v. Northamptonshire (Peterborough) 1934.

HAROLD LARWOOD
b 14.11.1904
Nottinghamshire and England

CAREER IN FIRST-CLASS CRICKET

				5 WKTS.	10 WKTS.
	RUNS	WKTS.	AVGE.	INNINGS	MATCH
1924	71	1	71.00	–	–
1925	1,315	73	18.01	3	1
1926	2,509	137	18.31	7	1
1927	1,695	100	16.95	8	3
1928	2,003	138	14.51	9	1
1928–29 (Aust.)	1,258	40	31.45	2	–
1929	2,535	117	21.66	6	1
1930	1,622	99	16.38	9	1
1931	1,553	129	12.03	12	2
1932	2,084	162	12.86	15	5
1932–33 (Aust.)	817	49	16.67	3	1
1933	18	1	18.00	–	–
1934	1,415	82	17.25	6	–
1935	2,316	102	22.70	2	–
1936	1,544	119	12.97	13	4
1936–37 (India)	157	2	78.50	–	–
1937	1,720	70	24.57	3	–
1938	366	6	61.00	–	–
	24,998	1,427	17.51	98	20

Cricket: The Great Bowlers

CAREER IN TEST CRICKET

MATCHES	BALLS	MDNS.	RUNS	WKTS.	AVGE.	5 WKTS. INNINGS	10 WKTS. MATCH
21	4,969	167	2,216	78	28.41	4	1

DEBUT MATCH: Nottinghamshire v. Northamptonshire (Nottingham) 1924.
BEST BOWLING: Nine wickets in an innings (1).
9-41 Nottinghamshire v. Kent (Nottingham) 1931.
BEST BOWLING IN TEST CRICKET: 6-32 England v. Australia (Brisbane) 1928–29.
'HAT-TRICKS' (2): Nottinghamshire v. Cambridge University (Cambridge) 1926.
Nottinghamshire v. Glamorgan (Nottingham) 1931.

CLARENCE VICTOR GRIMMETT
b 25.12.1892
Wellington, Victoria, South Australia and Australia

CAREER IN FIRST-CLASS CRICKET

	RUNS	WKTS.	AVGE.	5 WKTS. INNINGS	10 WKTS. MATCH
NEW ZEALAND					
1911–12	116	4	29.00	–	–
1912–13	65	1	65.00	–	–
1913–14	498	17	29.29	–	–
AUSTRALIA					
1918–19	34	0	–	–	–
1920–21	110	1	110.00	–	–
1921–22	161	6	26.83	–	–
1922–23	50	2	25.00	–	–
1923–24	98	9	10.88	1	–
1924–25	1,300	59	22.03	8	1
1925–26	1,794	59	30.40	8	3
1926 (Eng.)	1,857	105	17.68	7	1
1926–27	1,030	30	34.33	2	–

Statistics 181

	RUNS	WKTS.	AVGE.	5 WKTS. INNINGS	10 WKTS. MATCH
1927–28 (Aust.)	1,151	42	27.40	4	2
1927–28 (N.Z.)	795	47	16.91	5	1
1928–29	2,432	71	34.53	5	
1929–30	1,943	82	23.20	9	3
1930 (Eng.)	2,427	144	16.85	15	5
1930–31	1,417	74	19.14	7	1
1931–32	1,535	77	19.93	6	1
1932–33	1,577	55	28.67	5	1
1933–34	1,441	66	21.37	7	1
1934 (Eng.)	2,159	109	19.80	10	1
1934–35	1,215	58	20.94	6	3
1935–36 (S. Af.)	1,362	92	14.80	9	4
1936–37	1,443	48	30.06	1	–
1937–38	845	41	20.60	2	–
1938–39	563	27	20.85	2	1
1939–40	1,654	73	22.65	9	4
1940–41	668	25	26.72	1	–
	31,740	1,424	22.29	129	33

CAREER IN TEST CRICKET

MATCHES	BALLS	MDNS.	RUNS	WKTS.	AVGE.	5 WKTS. INNINGS	10 WKTS. MATCH
37	14,573	734	5,231	216	24.21	21	7

DEBUT MATCH: Wellington *v.* Auckland (Wellington) 1911–12.
BEST BOWLING: Ten wickets in an innings (1).
              Nine wickets in an innings (2).
              10-37 Australians *v.* Yorkshire (Sheffield) 1930.
              9-74 Australians *v.* Cambridge University (Cambridge) 1934.
              9-180 South Australia *v.* Queensland (Adelaide) 1934–35.
BEST BOWLING IN TEST CRICKET: 7-40 Australia *v.* South Africa (Johannesburg) 1935–36.
'HAT-TRICKS' (1): South Australia *v.* Queensland (Brisbane) 1928–29.

WILLIAM JOSEPH O'REILLY
b 20.12.1905
New South Wales and Australia

CAREER IN FIRST-CLASS CRICKET

	RUNS	WKTS.	AVGE.	5 WKTS. INNINGS	10 WKTS. MATCH
1927–28	189	7	27.00	–	–
1931–32	697	32	21.78	3	1
1932–33	1,237	62	19.95	5	1
1933–34	860	38	22.63	3	2
1934 (Eng.)	1,858	109	17.04	6	3
1934–35	251	8	31.37	–	–
1935–36 (Aust.)	56	5	11.20	–	–
1935–36 (S. Af.)	1,289	95	13.56	11	3
1936–37	1,052	51	20.62	3	–
1937–38	784	64	12.25	6	2
1938 (Eng.)	1,726	104	16.59	9	2
1938–39	440	19	23.15	2	1
1939–40	832	55	15.12	6	2
1940–41	684	55	12.43	5	–
1941–42	124	9	13.77	1	–
1945–46 (Aust.)	474	33	14.36	1	–
1945–46 (N.Z.)	297	28	10.60	2	–
	12,850	774	16.60	63	17

CAREER IN TEST CRICKET

MATCHES	BALLS	MDNS.	RUNS	WKTS.	AVGE.	5 WKTS. INNINGS	10 WKTS. MATCH
27	10,024	585	3,254	144	22.59	11	3

DEBUT MATCH: New South Wales *v.* New Zealanders (Sydney) 1927–28.
BEST BOWLING: Nine wickets in an innings (3).
9-38 Australians *v.* Somerset (Taunton) 1934.
9-41 New South Wales *v.* South Australia (Adelaide) 1937–38.
9-50 New South Wales *v.* Victoria (Melbourne) 1933–34.

BEST BOWLING IN TEST CRICKET: 7-54 Australia v. England (Nottingham) 1934.
'HAT-TRICKS': Nil.

RAYMOND RUSSELL LINDWALL, M.B.E.
b 3.10.1921
New South Wales, Queensland and Australia
CAREER IN FIRST-CLASS CRICKET

	RUNS	WKTS.	AVGE.	5 WKTS. INNINGS	10 WKTS. MATCH
1941–42	117	3	39.00	–	–
1945–46 (Aust.)	793	33	24.03	1	–
1945–46 (N.Z.)	259	9	28.77	–	–
1946–47	861	39	22.07	3	1
1947–48	616	29	21.24	1	–
1948 (Eng.)	1,349	86	15.68	6	1
1948–49	803	41	19.58	1	–
1949–50 (S. Af.)	729	50	14.58	2	–
1950–51	1,072	41	26.14	–	–
1951–52	728	42	17.33	2	–
1952–53	1,077	58	18.56	2	–
1953 (Eng.)	1,394	85	16.40	5	–
1953–54	663	22	30.13	1	–
1954–55 (Aust.)	584	22	26.54	–	–
1954–55 (W.I.)	808	28	28.85	2	–
1955–56	869	30	28.96	1	–
1956 (Eng.)	924	47	19.65	1	–
1956–57 (Pak. and India)	263	13	20.23	1	–
1956–57 (Aust.)	641	27	23.74	2	–
1957–58	670	26	25.76	1	–
1958–59	822	40	20.55	1	–
1959–60 (Pak. and India)	464	15	30.93	–	–
1959–60 (Aust.)	150	2	75.00	–	–
1960–61 (N.Z.)	22	0	–	–	–

	RUNS	WKTS.	AVGE.	5 WKTS. INNINGS	10 WKTS. MATCH
1960–61 (W.I.)	184	5	36.80	–	–
1961–62 (International XI Tour)	100	1	100.00	–	–
	16,962	794	21.36	33	2

CAREER IN TEST CRICKET

MATCHES	BALLS	MDNS.	RUNS	WKTS.	AVGE.	5 WKTS. INNINGS	10 WKTS. MATCH
61	13,666	417	5,257	228	23.05	12	–

DEBUT MATCH: New South Wales *v.* Queensland (Brisbane) 1941–42.
BEST BOWLING: 7-20 Australians *v.* Minor Counties (Stoke-on-Trent) 1953. Lindwall took seven wickets in an innings on six other occasions.
BEST BOWLING IN TEST CRICKET: 7-38 Australia *v.* India (Adelaide) 1947–48.
'HAT-TRICKS': Nil.

ALEC VICTOR BEDSER, O.B.E.
b 4.7.1918
Surrey and England

CAREER IN FIRST-CLASS CRICKET

	RUNS	WKTS.	AVGE.	5 WKTS. INNINGS	10 WKTS. MATCH
1939	59	0	–	–	–
1946	2,577	128	20.13	10	3
1946–47 (Aust. and N.Z.)	1,669	47	35.51	–	–
1947	3,175	130	24.42	6	1
1948	2,632	115	22.88	6	1
1948–49 (S. Af.)	1,273	45	28.28	1	–
1949	2,344	110	21.30	5	–

Statistics 185

	RUNS	WKTS.	AVGE.	5 WKTS. INNINGS	10 WKTS. MATCH
1950	2,797	122	22.92	6	1
1950–51 (Aust. and N.Z.)	1,148	53	21.66	3	1
1951	2,024	130	15.56	9	2
1952	2,530	154	16.42	10	1
1953	2,702	162	16.67	12	2
1954	1,828	121	15.10	5	1
1954–55 (Aust.)	659	24	27.45	1	–
1955	2,752	144	19.11	6	–
1956	1,950	96	20.31	4	1
1956–57 (India)	119	2	59.50	–	–
1957	2,170	131	16.56	4	1
1958	816	48	17.00	2	–
1959	2,208	91	24.26	3	–
1959–60 (Rhod.)	120	4	30.00	–	–
1960	1,729	67	25.80	3	1
	39,281	1,924	20.41	96	16

CAREER IN TEST CRICKET

MATCHES	BALLS	MDNS.	RUNS	WKTS.	AVGE.	5 WKTS. INNINGS	10 WKTS. MATCH
51	15,941	572	5,876	236	24.89	15	5

DEBUT MATCH: Surrey *v.* Oxford University (Oval) 1939.
BEST BOWLING: Eight wickets in an innings (4).
      8-18 Surrey *v.* Nottinghamshire (Oval) 1952.
      8-18 Surrey *v.* Warwickshire (Oval) 1953.
      8-42 Surrey *v.* Middlesex (Lord's) 1949.
      8-53 Surrey *v.* Leicestershire (Oval) 1950.
BEST BOWLING IN TEST CRICKET: 7-44 England *v.* Australia (Nottingham) 1953.
N.B. Bedser took 7-55 in the first innings of this match for a match analysis of 14-99.
'HAT-TRICKS' (1): Surrey *v.* Essex (Oval) 1953.

JAMES CHARLES LAKER
b 9.2.1922
Surrey, Essex and England
CAREER IN FIRST-CLASS CRICKET

	RUNS	WKTS.	AVGE.	5 WKTS. INNINGS	10 WKTS. MATCH
1946	169	8	21.12	–	–
1947	1,420	79	17.97	5	–
1947–48 (W.I.)	971	36	26.97	3	–
1948	2,903	104	27.91	4	–
1949	2,422	122	19.85	8	1
1950	2,544	166	15.32	12	5
1950–51 (India)	579	36	16.08	3	–
1951	2,681	149	17.99	13	5
1951–52 (N.Z.)	379	24	15.79	3	1
1952	2,219	125	17.75	9	1
1953	2,366	135	17.52	7	1
1953–54 (W.I.)	756	22	34.36	–	–
1954	2,048	135	15.17	13	5
1955	2,382	133	17.90	9	3
1956	1,906	132	14.43	8	3
1956–57 (S. Af.)	875	50	17.50	2	–
1957	1,921	126	15.24	5	–
1958	1,651	116	14.23	7	2
1958–59 (Aust.)	655	38	17.23	3	1
1959	1,920	78	24.61	5	2
1962	962	51	18.86	5	1
1963	828	43	19.25	2	1
1963–64 (W.I.)	221	5	44.20	–	–
1964	577	17	33.94	–	–
1964–65 (W.I.)	434	14	31.00	1	–
	35,789	1,944	18.40	127	32

CAREER IN TEST CRICKET

MATCHES	BALLS	MDNS.	RUNS	WKTS.	AVGE.	5 WKTS. INNINGS	10 WKTS. MATCH
46	12,009	673	4,099	193	21.23	9	3

DEBUT MATCH: Surrey *v.* Combined Services (Oval) 1946.

BEST BOWLING: Ten wickets in an innings (2):
Nine wickets in an innings (1):
10-53 England v. Australia (Manchester) 2nd innings, 1956.
10-88 Surrey v. Australians (Oval) 1956.
9-37 England v. Australia (Manchester) 1st innings, 1956.

N.B. Laker's match analysis of 19-90 against Australia at Manchester is the only instance in first-class cricket of a bowler taking 19 wickets in a match.

'HAT-TRICKS' (4): Sir Pelham Warner's XI v. South of England (Hastings) 1947.
Surrey v. Gloucestershire (Oval) 1951.
Surrey v. Warwickshire (Oval) 1953.
Surrey v. Cambridge University (Guildford) 1953.

FREDERICK SEWARDS TRUEMAN
b 6.2.1931
Yorkshire and England
CAREER IN FIRST-CLASS CRICKET

	RUNS	WKTS.	AVGE.	5 WKTS. INNINGS	10 WKTS. MATCH
1949	719	31	23.19	1	–
1950	876	31	28.25	–	–
1951	1,852	90	20.57	6	1
1952	841	61	13.78	5	–
1953	1,411	44	32.06	2	1
1953–54 (W.I.)	909	27	33.66	1	–
1954	2,085	134	15.55	10	–
1955	2,454	153	16.03	8	3
1956	1,383	59	23.44	2	–
1956–57 (India)	204	8	25.50	–	–
1957	2,303	135	17.05	9	2
1958	1,414	106	13.33	6	–
1958–59 (Aust. and N.Z.)	1,067	57	18.71	4	1
1959	2,730	140	19.50	6	–

188 Cricket: The Great Bowlers

	RUNS	WKTS.	AVGE.	5 WKTS. INNINGS	10 WKTS. MATCH
1959–60 (W.I.)	883	37	23.86	2	–
1960	2,447	175	13.98	12	4
1960–61 (S. Af.)	326	22	14.81	1	–
1961	3,000	155	19.35	11	4
1962	2,717	153	17.75	5	1
1962–63 (Aust. and N.Z.)	1,020	55	18.54	4	1
1963	1,955	129	15.15	10	5
1963–64 (W.I.)	124	9	13.77	–	–
1964	2,194	100	21.94	3	–
1964–65 (W.I.)	253	11	23.00	1	–
1965	1,811	127	14.25	10	1
1966	2,040	111	18.37	2	1
1967	1,610	75	21.46	2	–
	40,628	2,235	18.17	123	25

CAREER IN TEST CRICKET

MATCHES	BALLS	MDNS.	RUNS	WKTS.	AVGE.	5 WKTS. INNINGS	10 WKTS. MATCH
67	15,178	522	6,625	307	21.57	17	3

DEBUT MATCH: Yorkshire v. Cambridge University (Cambridge) 1949.
BEST BOWLING: Eight wickets in an innings (10).
    8-28 Yorkshire v. Kent (Dover) 1954.
    8-31 England v. India (Leeds) 1952.
    8-36 Yorkshire v. Sussex (Hove) 1965.
    8-37 Yorkshire v. Essex (Bradford) 1966.
    8-45 M.C.C. v. Otago (Dunedin) 1958–59.
    8-45 Yorkshire v. Gloucestershire (Bradford) 1963.
    8-53 Yorkshire v. Nottinghamshire (Nottingham) 1951.
    8-68 Yorkshire v. Nottinghamshire (Sheffield) 1951.
    8-70 Yorkshire v. Minor Counties (Lord's) 1949.
    8-84 Yorkshire v. Nottinghamshire (Worksop) 1962.
'HAT-TRICKS' (4): Yorkshire v. Nottinghamshire (Nottingham) 1951.
    Yorkshire v. Nottinghamshire (Scarborough) 1955.
    Yorkshire v. M.C.C. (Lord's) 1958.
    Yorkshire v. Nottinghamshire (Bradford) 1963.

JOHN BRIAN STATHAM, C.B.E.
b 17.6.1930
Lancashire and England
CAREER IN FIRST-CLASS CRICKET

	RUNS	WKTS.	AVGE.	5 WKTS. INNINGS	10 WKTS. MATCH
1950	613	37	16.56	2	–
1950–51 (Aust. and N.Z.)	220	11	20.00	–	–
1951	1,466	97	15.11	6	–
1951–52 (India and Pak.)	803	40	20.07	–	–
1952	1,989	110	18.08	2	–
1953	1,650	101	16.33	3	–
1953–54 (W.I.)	541	22	24.59	–	–
1954	1,300	92	14.13	6	–
1954–55 (Aust. and N.Z.)	916	54	16.96	2	–
1955	1,573	108	14.56	8	1
1956	1,351	91	14.84	5	–
1956–57 (S. Af.)	607	36	16.86	1	–
1957	1,895	126	15.03	7	1
1958	1,648	134	12.29	10	1
1958–59 (Aust.)	549	28	19.60	2	–
1959	2,087	139	15.01	6	1
1959–60 (W.I.)	493	15	32.86	–	–
1960	1,662	135	12.31	10	3
1960–61 (S. Af.)	240	21	11.42	2	–
1961	2,107	104	20.25	4	–
1962	2,207	102	21.63	3	–
1962–63 (Aust.)	1,043	33	31.60	–	–
1963	1,874	113	16.58	8	1
1964	2,203	110	20.03	6	1
1965	1,716	137	12.52	14	1
1966	1,479	102	14.50	7	1
1967	1,530	92	16.63	7	–
	35,762	2,190	16.32	121	11

CAREER IN TEST CRICKET

MATCHES	BALLS	MDNS.	RUNS	WKTS.	AVGE.	5 WKTS. INNINGS	10 WKTS. MATCH
70	16,026	590	6,257	252	24.82	9	1

DEBUT MATCH: Lancashire v. Kent (Manchester) 1950.
BEST BOWLING: Eight wickets in an innings (4).
    8-34 Lancashire v. Warwickshire (Coventry) 1957.
    8-37 Lancashire v. Leicestershire (Leicester) 1964.
    8-44 Lancashire v. Nottinghamshire (Manchester) 1959.
    8-69 Lancashire v. Gloucestershire (Manchester) 1965.
BEST BOWLING IN TEST CRICKET: 7-39 England v. South Africa (Lord's) 1955.
'HAT-TRICKS' (3): Lancashire v. Sussex (Manchester) 1956.
    M.C.C. v. Transvaal (Johannesburg) 1956–57.
    Lancashire v. Leicestershire (Manchester) 1958.